Jen Knox is an exceptionally gifted events of the past and craft them in compelling narratives.

—**Phillip Lopate, author of** *Notes*

With her unique voice, Jen tells the poignant, yet raw, story of her journey to adulthood, living on the streets as a runaway and her ultimate struggle to establish her own identity as a woman who truly values herself. This is one of those books that lingers long after the last page.

—**Heather McIntosh, author of** *Small Animals First*

Jen's a runner, a runaway. Following in the footsteps of her great grandmother, Glory, who defiantly set out on her own near the same young age, and finding commonalities of mental illnesses among the women in her family, Jen must've realized her course was set out for her organically.

In the writing of *Musical Chairs*, a memoir blatant and unapologetic, Jen attempts to make sense of herself within the larger family history. Yet, for all of the similarities Jen discovered between herself and Glory, there is at least one difference: Glory ran away from family, while Jen's running brought the both of them back.

—**Jennifer Lynne Roberts, playwright and writer, author of** *Beekeeper* **and** *Book of Taos*

This true tale of grit, survival and eventual rebirth of the psyche is engaging and inspirational, even to a small-town girl like me.

—**Gretchen A. Phillips, Pearson Education**

Musical Chairs

Jen Knox

Musical Chairs
Copyright © 2009 by Jennifer Knox

Musical Chairs is a memoir. It reflects the author's sincere recollection
and analysis of her personal experiences. Certain names, specific
locations and identifying characteristics have been altered. All events
have been recreated from memory, and, in some cases, have been
compressed to convey the essence of what occurred.

ISBN 13: 978-0-9842594-2-7
Library of Congress Control Number: 2009909867

Cover Photo by: Mark R. Knox, KnoxworX Studios

Cover Design by All Things That Matter Press
Published in 2009 by All Things That Matter Press

I want to dedicate this book to Grandma Gloria, Mom, Dad and Laura, thank you for endless support and unconditional love.

To my husband and the B&C combo, thank you, for always being there.

Thank you, also, to my teachers, mentors, readers and my writing family, for helping me understand the value of words and the beauty and importance of personal stories.

Table of Contents

PROLOGUE

Throughout the summer of 2003 I repeatedly underwent what psychologists have since diagnosed as post-traumatic stress and panic disorder. A spiritually-inclined friend refers to the same summer as my rebirthing period. Still others, who claim to have had similar experiences, tell me that such episodes were probably a warning, my body's way of telling me to adopt healthier eating habits, exercise more or quit smoking. At the time, all I knew was that the onset was swift.

I was working at a bookstore in Upper Arlington, a suburb of Columbus, Ohio. The store was small, quiet. Gently modulating harmonies, barely audible, filled the vast empty space between customers as I perused the alphabet of author names in front of me, searching for a paperback's designated spot. I had made it my goal to shelve the last two stacks of romance novels before taking a break, and I was on target, moving industriously until I reached to shelve one of the last titles and my arm went slack, my fingers released. But the book didn't fall.

I could see my hand, pale and bony with soft freckles dotting knuckles, fingers still wrapped around the book's yellow spine. I turned the hand over, tracing its outline in my mind, trying to understand why I could no longer feel the silken texture of the cover. The sensation I felt was almost peaceful at first; it was as though I were wandering through my body, haunting and examining but unable to control it. I waited a moment for the cohesion of normalcy, but it wouldn't come and soon my mind turned restless, flooding with possible causation: aneurism, stroke, heart attack, sudden death syndrome. I had visions of collapsing to the ground, of medics trying to resuscitate me. I began to hear pulsing fluids moving inside me. I was overwhelmed by a desire to run in every direction at once.

A stooped woman dressed in gray and light blue approached me slowly, asked me to help her find the history section of the store. Her light eyes, sheathed with experience, seemed to mock me, laugh at my wretched vulnerability, my dispensable life. I wondered at the superiority of her years; what had she done to deserve them? What could she teach me?

"Miss? I asked you a question," she said.

I felt the vibration of chords and soft tissue in my neck as my voice directed her to the wall opposite and, without waiting for a response, I walked away. I felt as though I were being led by my own body, each step ethereal but swift, limbs moving involuntarily. Two size fives in closed-toe shoes were leading the way—they had navigated this path before. When I was alone in the break room, my body turned its back to a chair and my knees bent slowly until the backs of my legs met the gold and green upholstery. This is when the lack of sensation changed, and, suddenly, I became hyperaware.

I squirmed, trying to escape the sounds: the clicks of another's hand entering a code, the vending machine grumbling beside me and lightly shaking the chair in which I sat. The vent above me thumped inharmoniously with my body's rhythm as it bucked a miasma of stale air into the room. My mouth seemed overly warm and the contrast of wet tissues and smooth tooth enamel repelled my tongue. The smallness of the room, closing in, suffocated my eyes with artificial light that fell on worn beige walls, a checkered tablecloth that caused my head to spin. My skin prickled as though small needles were entering each pore. Just as the door opened, my eyes closed and the needles all burrowed beneath my epidermis and swam through my body to my chest where they extracted the air from my lungs and stopped my heart.

Co-workers huddled around, asking me what was wrong. I was hunched over in the chair with my head between my legs, shaking now, and unable to explain. All I knew was that my body was failing, and I didn't want this audience. My chest contracted each time I struggled to take a full breath so that I could only gasp when I tried to respond to questions. I tried to ignore the audience, but when I closed my eyes the cold air grip that was suffocating my skin grew stronger, squeezing.

What comes after was akin to a blackout, and I can only see clips of the events that followed. My manager drove me to the emergency room, and I became conscious of her nervous irritation at traffic lights and her tired, worried gaze as it lingered on me. I sat like a nervous child, holding one knee to my chest as I fixed my eyes on the dull burgundy glove compartment in front of me. When we arrived at the emergency room, it was my manager who explained that I might be having a heart or asthma attack; she said this to someone at a desk who immediately had me ushered back to a sterile, semi-private room.

I was rigid, sitting on the edge of a bed, cringing as nurses took samples of my blood, pushing needles into my skin while stating things like "You sure have stubborn veins. Try pumping your fist again." They said they were testing for signs of everything from pregnancy to irregular levels of glucose and minerals. I concentrated only on my breath, trying to control it as these nurses entered and left my room in a haze of loud scrubs and soft voices, leaving cups for me to fill with urine and telling me to relax. Surprisingly, in the midst of all the chaos, I did. I became amiable as they asked me questions, passing my chart like a game of tag. I tried my best to answer their questions about my pain.

Anxious to hear my diagnosis, I felt another wave of relief when the doctor finally arrived. I noticed that his posture was impeccable, almost awkward when contrasted to the urgent forward-tilt of the nurse who followed him in. He held a file with my name on it. As he flipped through pages, I sat up straight, bracing myself.

"You're in good shape," he began. I waited. "Your lungs are clear and you have a rather slow heart rate, which is a good thing. You couldn't ask for better numbers on your blood pressure…." He ran down the series of test results. "We don't have all your blood work, of course, but it looks like you just had a panic attack."

My displeasure with this answer must have been evident because he immediately defended his diagnosis. "We get quite a few cases of panic every day. You'd be surprised what stress can do. Are you under a lot of stress?"

"No," I said flatly.

"Ms. Knox, my advice is to take a close look at your lifestyle. Stressors can take different forms, and sometimes they're hard to identify; sometimes even positive things can cause stress, such as a new relationship or college finals." I wasn't convinced. I would have understood if this had happened five years ago, but at the time my life was remarkably tranquil. The doctor handed me a referral with the number of a psychologist, handed my file to a nurse, and rushed off to patients who were actually sick.

Why the initial aversion to the doctor's diagnosis? Well, for starters, it's not pleasant to hear that you're imagining your own pain or that it's the self-inflicted sort. Moreover, both sides of my family tree are laden with the gamut of mental illness; and, at the time of my attack, I was in the midst of re-establishing a relationship with my schizophrenic grandmother. As I sought to find reason, to guard myself against another attack, I was being introduced to a paradigm view of our family's tradition of madness, a tradition I'd long feared would trickle down to me, and one I'd long hoped I might elude. I wondered whether I might have absorbed some of Grandma's insanity through osmosis. Our relationship was burgeoning into the mutual dependency of family, and I couldn't help considering that I restrict the absurd amount of time we were spending together.

In defense of this rather cold introduction to my grandmother, the woman had a unique and uncanny way of enraging me. It wasn't just her cutting insults or her vague delusions about the world, but her sheer inconsistency that was most disturbing. She would be chatty and articulate one minute, and then her eyes would shift and her sermons of gloom and foolishness would begin. She believed, for instance, that she had been the cause of the first Iraq war because she ate her eggs poached instead of scrambled; she often turned over her chairs and tables, covering them in sheets when they began to look "menacing;" she claimed to see codes in news programs (she knew what it had *really* meant that the news anchor had worn blue); she regularly told me that the United States were falling apart and I had better watch out for "The Chinese." Some days she called me just to tell me not to leave home; other days she insisted I come over "urgently," then scolded me when I showed up wearing sweats, put on some tea and said she'd just like to chat about the goings-on.

Despite all the above and my irrational fear that she was contagious, I was eager to prove myself capable of dealing with Grandma, primarily because I was her only nearby mobile family member. Also, I was trying to regain the respect of my father who had entrusted me with the task.

There were days that Grandma was a pleasant conversationalist. And she always had some kind of cookies and tea to offer, which I found a rare and endearing gesture. Over the course of this summer, in fact, Grandma began to tell me stories about our family, most of whom I had never met. Her tales would prove enlightening, disturbing and mysterious.

I heard tales of my great-grandmother, Glory, whom I immediately became enamored with. I grew up hearing my parents' warnings that Glory was an angry, spiteful, dried-up old woman who spent the last of her ninety-two years in California alone so that she could avoid us, her family. When I was a child, I thought of her as the older women in Disney movies who wore dark cloaks and unkempt hairstyles, who always wanted to destroy everything around them. She was the villainous legend, and my grandmother was—this, according to my father—her victim.

"You look a lot like her," Grandma told me. "And you ran away from home at fifteen, just like her. That's kind of strange, huh?" Although I wasn't sure how to take this observation, I found it incredibly interesting. I asked if Glory had panic, anxiety, and she thought. "Well, I doubt that, but I suppose it's possible. She did get the urge to move around a lot."

Grandma began to incorporate her own past in short but vivid scenes starring Glory, and, in this way, I began to learn about both women. I began to construct a different portrait of my family, one that made my own panic seem less important, less lonesome. It's fascinating now to think that it was the very woman who enraged me, who suffers so thoroughly from her own distress, taught me to face my own panic. That summer, as the stories of my family began to surface, I began to realize that it was only a matter of time before I faced my own.

I, too, was fifteen when I ran away from home, driven by a menacing craving that Glory might have understood. I have one picture of myself in the midst of my years as a runaway. I appear hungry. There is a clean side part in my hair; my sunken-in cheeks are accented by severe, dark blush; my skinny shoulder peeks out from an over-sized shirt. I am holding myself up, barely, leaning against a bathroom sink. I stare somewhere beyond the camera, too numb for the panic that would grip me years later. Beside me are two girls, their slender, sequin-covered arms wrapped around me. Now, as I attempt to trace the jagged lines of the past through memory and perspective, I can comfortably say that a summer filled with panic was inevitable.

PART ONE:

THE RUNAWAY

Home

I remember racing my sister toward High Street. We would just miss the bus that approached across the gravel lot by our back porch. Not that we had bus money or a place to go, but it was fun to try, to imagine stealing off into the world, to begin our adult lives. The big grey COTA bus would spit smoke at us and ease away.

High Street was filled with vacant buildings then, and those that were inhabited specialized in used furniture or repairs; these shops sat alongside pawnshops and a few small restaurants and bars. Close to downtown with highly publicized crime and the nearby pockets of affluence, our neighborhood, as a whole, had an eerie glamour; it was teetering on the verge of extremes. The Columbus Police, over-burdened with calls to our stretch of land between downtown Columbus and the Ohio State University nicknamed the neighborhood the *Short North* around the time my parents moved there in 1980. I was less than a year old.

Our home, an old rooming house, was in the heart of the Short North. It was what my father liked to call "a fixer-upper." The bare brick walls in the kitchen and directly above, in my bedroom, made the place drafty in the winter and cool in the summer. My father remembers his excitement, seeing the promise of the place long before it was realized, and it turns out his investment and timing would prove incredibly savvy twenty years later. Throughout my childhood, however, I can't say it was a house worth bragging about.

A grubby squad of homeless men came to inhabit our backyard, guarding it, they promised, against robberies in exchange for the territory. It was usually the same three sun-roughened men in faded clothes. Dad sometimes asked for the men's assistance tearing down walls or painting rooms in the house. In exchange, he always offered food or drink, never cash. My father would sit on the back stoop and listen to stories about life on the streets.

Had a passerby not known my father, there would have been no reason to think him the owner of our home. My father rarely purchased new clothing and often his pants would be speckled with paint or dotted with pen marks. He was an artist who experimented with all mediums and rarely changed from his work clothes. Moreover, he wore his Asics until they "spoke," the rubber flapping like a floppy mouth opening and closing with each step. My father—a middle-aged hippie with long, dark hair and a lingering inclination to hit a pipe of hashish, but only when the children were sound asleep—had the respect of these men, many of whom were Vietnam vets.

I feared these men at first, but any trepidation was squashed with my father's assurance that they were "good men with bad breaks." Nonetheless, I suspect that my father had asked them to keep their distance from me and my sister because the men rarely engaged either of us in conversation. Outside of asking when my father would be home or the offering of a friendly hello, I rarely saw an eye bat my way. When I was instructed to take the trash out, which meant walking directly through their hangout, they would only nod and smile as I passed. If the bag was especially heavy, when I struggled, one of the men might approach, to help me push the trash into the tall dumpster. I would thank the man and wave goodbye shyly before running back home, my stomach aflutter.

I began to imagine that they were our guardian angels. I would watch them from my bedroom window, wonder what they talked about over silver cans of beer; sometimes my father would share bits of his conversations with us over dinner, and I enjoyed these stories. When the Columbus Police waged war on Short North crime, it meant trouble for our backyard residents. Dad complained that the police bothered his friends instead of going after real criminals elsewhere, criminals that they were afraid of. Many of the men were arrested or warned to move on. They weren't even allowed to sleep behind the UDF down the street, their other hangout. Perhaps my memory is imposing coincidence, or maybe this is just around the time I began to notice what was already happening inside our home, but I mark the departure of these men as the beginning of my family's disjointing, and my own discomfort on Mt. Pleasant Avenue.

Over the course of ensuing years, our house had been divvied up between my parents. It had been a gradual process, but one that my younger sister and I predicted. Eagerly, we waited for divorce, and by the end of the eighties, we were old enough to begin betting on how long it would take. Laura would sneak out onto the ledge outside my room and knock; her rainbow of Kool-Aid-dyed hair pulled into a ponytail that extended down her back. We would sit there on either side of the window and discuss the matter seriously, wondering if we could do anything that would hurry the process along. Our parents battled each other with silence and avoidance, but I often wished for screaming or actual arguments that I could hear. The silence was suffocating, and, worse, it left nothing to complain about at length.

While Laura and I found sanctuary in our rooms, Dad usually claimed the backroom and basement, where he worked on his drawings. Or he kept busy repairing things around the house. Mom maintained primary residency in the kitchen and on the front porch. Their worlds were separate, distinct. Only dinner, or a third party, such as one of us kids or a neighbor, could keep them in the same room for more than a passing minute.

Beyond cooking, Mom's claim to the kitchen was easy access to the phone. Our cordless was Mom's portal to the outside world and it got the best reception there in the kitchen, by the brick wall where she smoked. Mom's conversations seemed to free her, take her to a different world that I wanted to know more about. Laura and I would joke about Mom needing surgery—to get the light, blue phone removed from her ear.

"Smart-asses," she would say, then laugh and laugh.

I often ran to answer it when it rang, and, almost as often, the same man with a southern voice cooed into my ear, "Hey, sweetie, where's your Momma at?"

"I'll get her. Who may I ask is calling?"

"Just tell her someone needs some guidance." I recognized the voice. Another time I asked for his name he chose to respond as "having issues only Miss Anita could help him with," and the time before that he asked for "your angel of a mother."

"Mom! It's that guy with issues again," I yelled from the hallway, down toward the kitchen. I waited, listening to the phone.

Her voice arrived. "Hi sweetie, how are you holding up?" I hung up.

Many of Mom's friends spoke about "sponsors" and "issues" and "guidance" during the times I listened in on the calls. And I wondered how much Mom could actually do for these people. She wasn't all that good at fixing issues at home. When Dad said something in our house it was always the final word, the loudest word, the longest word. So why were all these men and women calling and asking for the very same thing she didn't do here? I resolved to ask.

I waited until a Saturday, when Laura and Dad were at the YMCA and Mom and I were alone, a rarity. Pee Wee Herman bounced around his colorful living room and Mom had just hung up after a long, soft-voiced call.

Without moving, I said, "Mom, can we talk?"

"Chairey," Mom exclaimed, eyes on the large chair that sang toward the smiling man in the gray suit.

"Mom, seriously,"

"Of course, sweetie. It's a pretty day, let's go outside."

I followed her and hopped up onto the porch swing my father had whipped up one summer with lumber and a thick chain. Mom sat on the step just below me. Her hair was dark at that time, curly, and thick. I liked to push my fingers through it when we sat next to each other to watch TV.

She breathed out heavily and then reached for a Benson & Hedges Menthol Ultra Light. "What's on your mind?" she asked seriously.

I hesitated. I should've thought out what I wanted to say. "Umm… what's a sponsor?"

She took a long drag, and looked at me, considering my question with an adult-to-adult regard. I appreciated this. "You mean Gregory?"

I shrugged. "I just want to know what you always talk about on the phone. You know, like what a sponsor means…."

Her cheeks drew inward as she blew out a thin cloud of smoke. I hoped I hadn't said anything wrong. "How would you like to take a trip with me tonight, to my meeting?"

I was shocked. This was an invitation into my mother's secret world. "Uh, okay."

"Okay. It should answer your questions, hon."

"Okay, yeah!" I said, as I hopped off the creaking swing. It was going to be just her and me. This was a rare and beautiful opportunity. I searched through my closet for the perfect outfit. I had a lot of spandex pants for running around in, and racing shirts. I also had an Easter dress from the year before. Unfortunately, I didn't have much in between. I decided to settle on jeans and a race shirt that said *The Tomato Town Trot*, which I stylishly tucked in. At the very least, it would advertise the fact that I could run five miles at a young age. Then, to kick up my look, I added a pair of gold-colored earrings that I had bought at the dollar store. They were big loops with beads that moved around whenever I moved my head. I slid down the stairs on my butt, and Mom met me at the bottom.

"Well, don't you look pretty," she smiled at me as she said this.

"The lipstick is too bright," Laura added as she put down her gym bag. I was upset that she was home. Her green hair was fading, probably a result of the chlorine at the YMCA pool. I waved Laura's opinion off as though it were flying too close to my face.

"Jealous," I hissed.

"When do you plan on coming home?" Dad wanted to know. He was asking Mom. He seemed irritated.

"We'll be home when we're home," she said. Mom led me out of the house, out of the tense air, the always tense air. Just going out with Mom was strange and exciting. Usually, my father was the one to take me — anywhere. If there were any mother-daughter bonding moments, they would be shared between my sister and my mother. Maybe this trip would change the dynamic. I smirked as Laura followed us. She stayed at our heels until we reached the door; she was begging to come, but Mom said she wasn't old enough to go. Ha!

I watched familiar art shops and bars around our home give way to small, cozy residential homes and cow pastures. I fidgeted with my seat belt as I looked around, curious as to where we would turn next. I rarely got to ride in the front passenger seat of the White Rabbit, our car. I reached for Mom's Pepsi can. "That's my ashtray, Jen. We'll get you something to drink soon." As Mom lit a skinny cigarette, I inhaled deeply.

"I thought you were going to quit," I said.

"I just said that so your father would stop lecturing me about it, to be honest, honey." I listened to her sharp inhale and slow release of smoke. "But I will quit. Is the smoke bothering you?" I said no.

We passed more homes, all of which began to look the same, squat, light-colored bungalows. Bored by the view, I began asking Mom questions. Was I dressed okay? Are there any topics that might impress her secret friends? Would we be gone long? Did we have to go back? Could we get dessert after? She waited patiently and then asked if I was quite finished asking questions. After I promised that I was, she explained that the people we were going to see weren't *secret* friends, just people I hadn't met. And that the rest of my questions would be answered soon enough.

We pulled into a church parking lot. "Church? Really?"

Mom looked over at me and cupped my face as she explained, "The people in this place are recovering from drug and alcohol addictions. We all gather here to share our stories and help each other to stay clean." I tried to nod, to show I understood. I wanted nothing more than to meet her friends and make them my friends, too. I never once that day considered that my Mom might be at that meeting for her own support, as well. She was the caretaker, the force that made my bruises hurt less. She was the sponsor.

We walked into a large basement room with a tiled floor. There was a wall of smoke so thick that it almost camouflaged the doorway. Once inside, I needed a while for my eyes to adjust to the florescence. There was a table set up with coffee and cookies. There were many scrawny men and women, all with long cigarettes like Mom's. I felt nervous as I gazed around at them. All of them, it seemed, staring at me. Some of them looked ill; all of them looked somehow relieved. I kept my eyes on the white and grey speckled tiles.

"Is that Red?" The voice was familiar.

"Jane?"

I looked up, hoping I was right. "Hi!" I said, elated and relieved that I knew one of these adults, my "Aunt" Jane, Mom's best friend.

"Hi, baby. I like those earrings," she said. Jane was glamorous, a tall woman with hair that was redder than my own. She dazzled, ear to wrist, with matching diamonds.

"Thank you. I like yours. They remind me of Madonna's." That was a stupid thing to say, I told myself. My face flushed. She didn't notice.

"Very nice," she said and gave Mom a hug. "Come on, sweetie, let's find some seats." Jane led me to some of the few empty chairs in the room. "Hey, Jimmy, can you scoot for this lovely lady?"

"For a lady as lovely as that? Of course, but I didn't know you had a little one."

"This here is Anita's kid."

"Oh! Well, for Anita's kid, I'll scoot my butt over for sure. Sit down, kid. You know your Mom is a very special lady? I think she may even be an angel."

"Thank you," I said as I looked around the room, eager to see what would happen next.

"And what's your name?" the man asked. His brown eyes were wide, as were his smile and waistline. I told him my name quietly. He stuck out a rough hand and I looked up. My face grew red as I stuck out my hand to shake. "Listen, you're just in time for the speaker. We always have a speaker, usually Johnny. Then anyone who wants to can get up and talk about what's bothering them."

"That's it?"

"That's it."

"Are the cookies only for people who speak?"

The man chortled as though attempting to loosen something from his throat. He pulled out a cigarette and lit it. It dangled from his lip, stuck there by some invisible glue, bobbing as he talked. "Do you want chocolate chip or striped cookies?"

"Striped cookie," I said, looking around for Mom. There was a group of men and women surrounding her. "I'll get them," I told the man. "Will you save my seat?"

"Sure thing, princess."

"Thanks," I jumped up and rushed over to where Mom was, leaving Jane and Jimmy to talk. I tried to nudge against Mom, but she was too animated.

"Her father will just have to build a bridge and get over himself," Mom was saying, and everyone laughed. This was one of Mom's favorite phrases. *You're mad at your sister? Why are you telling me? Just build a bridge and get over it.* She patted me on the head as I pushed into her circle and smiles came down on me from the three other women and two men.

"Amen," a voice said.

I took three cookies and rushed back to my seat as an amplified voice filled the room. We all sat and one of the men who had been in my mom's circle took the podium.

"Hello. My name is Gregory and I'm an addict," he said.

The entire room responded to him, "Hello Gregory."

"We have all survived another beautiful Saturday. God knows, every day is a miracle."

"A miracle," a woman in the row behind me repeated.

The man continued, "I see a few new faces today." Uh-oh, I thought, please don't point me out. "I know that some of you may want to share your stories and some of you may not, but above all I want you all to know that we are here to support you. This is a room full of love and acceptance. This is a room of forgiveness. And this room is an opportunity for you to release the past and begin a new future. One step at a time."

Many people affirmed his statement, repeating it or piping up with a soft "Yes" or "That's right!"

"Thank you to Miss Sheila for bringing our snacks today. And thank you, Miss Anita, for providing the food for our picnic last week."

Mom gave Gregory a smile and nod.

"I surrender the mic. Who's up?" He scanned the room.

"Mom, are you going to speak?"

"Not today, honey."

Mom didn't have to speak that night. A crease of worry appeared on her face as others spoke. It was like that for everyone there. They seemed close, connected in a painful way. Some spoke of hurting other people and feeling horrible about it now; others spoke of hospital visits and addictive behavior they saw in their spouse or children. Why were they telling all these sad stories? Why not build a bridge and get over it?

By the end of the night, I began to realize that the people in that room had developed a special bond, not quite like family, but similar. As each person rose to speak, applause would spread throughout the room like an audible hug. The person would stand up there shakily and begin to tell a sad tale. Some of them were good storytellers, some weren't. They all had tears. And the more tears they shed, the more encouragement they would receive from the crowd.

I thought I would raise my hand after the last speaker and be the big finale. I would talk about school, and how I hated the other kids. Or the fact that my lizard died prematurely because I had forgotten to keep his lamp on, and lizards needed warmth to survive. I was sure I would get more hugs than all of them put together. When the last speaker was done, everyone rose to hug her and congratulate her on her courage. "One step at a time," Gregory said into the microphone, concluding the meeting. This was my last chance. I worked my hand up until it was level with the chairs in front of me. Mom shot me a look and I set it back in my lap. "Thanks for coming out tonight. If you are new today and you need a sponsor, get with me after this and we'll hook you up. We all need a sponsor in life, remember that. And thank you for the many people who came out and shared their stories with us today."

On the car ride home, I told Mom that I wanted to come again. I told her that I wanted to be a part of this group and she laughed. "But there are so many people who love each other and support each other."

"Honey, these people are all addicted to drugs and alcohol. That's why they need support."

"Well, what if someone had a sad story to tell, but it didn't have anything to do with drugs? Could that person still come to these meetings?"

"That would be pretty pathetic," Mom said. Then she corrected herself and smiled. She said I could come back with her anytime. I never did.

1994

My parents' divorce was not the easy split my sister and I had envisioned. It was financially messy and emotionally muddled. Mom didn't fight for any material possessions; consequently, she seemed to end up on the losing side of the division. I felt obliged to her during this time. My choice to take her "side" was romanticized by the fact that she was no longer around (the absent parent, the victim could do no wrong). She was living with her friend, Jane, while she saved enough money to get an apartment of her own, and in the meantime my father had primary custody of their rebellious teenage girls. Looking back, I feel nothing short of compassion for my father, but at the time I was too self-consumed to notice the challenge I was presenting to him.

Even then I had known Mom wouldn't fight. There was no reason to. My father didn't lose. Years before, when Laura and I were still wearing matching footed pajamas in secondary colors, long before the house became a series of territories and awkward conversations, my parents would often disappear into their bedroom for long periods of time. Laura and I would tiptoe up to the door, huddle in close, eager to hear what was going on. Our parents' muted discussions would occasionally refer back to familiar topics including money, goal-setting, and "the kids" (the subject of us would pique our interest just enough to cause us to listen for long periods of time). But eventually, my sister and I would grow bored and begin staring at each other, making faces, trying to get the other to giggle and blow our cover.

These conversations always began quietly but, as time passed, the voices would quicken and then Mom's would begin to weaken and ultimately disappear completely. They were not fighting. Rather, my father was lecturing, stating his facts. My sister's hazel eyes, the mirror image of her mother's, would narrow. I would study her face for a reaction, careful not to show my own.

We would exchange notes about what we'd heard, agreeing that Dad was rigid and wrong concerning his beliefs about us (these kids need to do more activities, more chores) and that his opinions and criticisms concerning Mom were simply obnoxious (you can do better than that job cooking at the mall, Anita, I only tell you to lose weight and quit smoking because I care about you, why don't you understand that? Let me explain…). They never got physical, but we could see a change in my mother when she walked out. She walked hunched over as I imagined a battered woman would, caught in a darker shade of reality, one shadowed by feelings of resignation, shame and defeat. "Your father sucks the lifeblood out of me" she'd say before going to sit on the front porch where she would chain-smoke. Laura would rush out after her, and I, inevitably, would get called by my father help with the dishes.

"Come on, get your spot journal. I'll let you rinse." My spot journal was a nice leather ledger with yellowing paper that was filled with an elaborate point system where I could record any spots my father left on the dishes after he washed. If it was a piece of food, worthy of passing back to him for a second wash, he'd give me a point. Two spots on the same dish would earn double the points, and the value would continue to grow, exponentially, with three and up. When I washed and he rinsed, I was at risk of losing points, so I always wanted to rinse. I grabbed the ledger and plopped it down on the sink as my father ran the dishwater.

He confided in me that he and Mom had argued. And, perhaps in order to dissipate the after effects of the argument, he gave me his biased rundown. He explained that he only tried to help Mom and he was baffled by her inability to realize this. I nodded along, fingering each dish under a steady stream of lukewarm water. "Spot," I called out. "Double spot," I corrected, quickly, before the dish reached my father's grip.

"There's a third spot on this dish. Cheese is tough to get off sometimes. Take that extra spot off your total. Record one point." These points equaled five cents each, and such misses were what kept me from really cashing in. I was saving up for modeling school and I had banked almost thirty dollars. Six hundred to go.

"She just seems so sad," he continued. "She never used to be like this."

After a moment of silence, Dad asked me how school had been going and offered to review my homework that was due on Monday. I had been working on a science project, which I had copied, lamely, from a book that suggested I mother three identical amaryllis plants, keeping one in a dark damp place, one in direct sunlight, and the last under artificial plant.

"I think you can do better than that," he said, suggesting I feed the plants interesting things, like the Maker's Mark he kept in the cabinet above the fridge, or milk or cola.

"That's cool, but I already started. The one under the sink is already wilting." My father shrugged this off, handing me one of the jelly jars we drank from. I inspected the rim, a good spot for small clusters of sugar or dried milk to collect.

"Let's do this. I'll pick you up some more plants after this. You want to do the best job you can on these projects. Some people out there in the world say that girls aren't as good at science at boys and you want to prove them wrong. You can't do things halfway."

"But the project is due Monday," I contested. The windows in the kitchen were all open and the sun washed over my father's pale face. I looked up at him, noticing the way his dark beard reflected a subtle reddish tint, similar to the color of my own hair.

"Let's just try it out anyway," he said. I said nothing. "While I'm at the store, I want you to vacuum. Maybe seeing that the dishes are clean, and the house looks good, your mother will lose the attitude."

Our kitchen was adorned with African masks and my father's art. When they were still dating, Dad drew Mom's body in sections, charcoal outlines of her thigh or the side of her arm, her waist, framed grayscale pictures. The portraits were a series of framed mysteries. I didn't understand their symbolism, and I remember searching for familiar lines in the shading. Only my parents knew which picture was the outline of a calf, the side of hip. I could only make out shapes.

When Mom came back in, she was reenergized, ready to say everything she couldn't say to him. "Well, thanks for cleaning," she told me. "Since *I* never do." With my father in earshot, she continued, "So, kids, you know what I learned today? I leaned that if *I* didn't spend so much money on *Ramen noodles* and *Hot Pockets* like we're having for dinner tonight, we could buy that bike Laura wanted for her birthday, but, hey, *I'm* a spendthrift. Oh, and I'm too fat, in case you didn't know." Laura and I sat at the kitchen table until Dad intervened, suggesting that Mom take us to our grandmother's apartment, a few blocks away, so that they could work things out "So that the kids won't be involved".

When Mom dropped us off, she would stay in the car and watch us as we rang the doorbell at the base of the two-apartment townhome. "Call me if you need to," she'd holler. We could hear Grandma clop down the stairs behind the door. When she would answer, usually with her cola colored hair half-covered with a sheer scarf, she would stand there a moment and look us up and down. Her bright makeup and pale complexion would seem to crack in half, exposing her tar-stained smile. Mom and my grandmother exchanged a forced wave and then my sister and I were on our own.

"I don't know why your mother never comes in for coffee," she'd always lie after assessing our choice of clothing. "Has she managed to lose any weight yet? I couldn't tell from all the way across the street."

"She doesn't need to," Laura would snap.

I had always thought my grandmother was a mildly cruel woman and I didn't want to go see her, ever, but I was beginning to realize that her cruelty was her sanest mood. Dad would insist that I develop a relationship with her, his mother, reminding me that she was merely a victim of her own mother's abuse and, subsequently, her mental illness. My sister and I would whine, but, to be fair, every visit had its high points: we would always get ice cream there, and sometimes she would tell our fortunes from tea leaves, or read us a part of *Treasure Island* or *Gulliver's Travels.* Then inevitably, something would shift in her mood.

Laura and I sat on the couch as Grandma Gloria paced that night, explaining, irritably, that we must write the absent numbers on the advertisement pages of her *Good Housekeeping* magazines so that there would be less crime on Wednesday. I ventured that this made no sense, but she was passionate about this assignment and insisted that it was imperative. "But I don't know what you want us to do."

She bent over me, her Chanel No. 5 so strong that I held my breath when she got too close. "This page, see," she pointed to a page with an advertisement on it for blue jeans. The girl in the picture had a clogged heel where the page number was supposed to be. "And this," she turned the page, and pointed to the number 56 in the lower corner. "This means that you need to write fifty-five right there." She pointed back to the woman's shoe.

"But why?"

"You just don't understand yet," she said, as though my misunderstanding was the thing that didn't make sense. I began to fear she may be right. "Now let's go get you ready for bed, then we'll eat, and then we'll get back to work on these. It's important, but you kids take forever to get ready."

Grandma dressed us up in matching frilly nightgowns with stiff lace collars. She said she bought them from Lazarus and that they were all ours—mine was blue, Laura's was pink—but we couldn't take them home yet.

She made us peanut butter and honey sandwiches on buttered toast. They melted delectably in our mouths before she had time to finish making her own. She boiled water for tea. The tea was too sweet and we would drink it as fast as possible. Grandma opened a small blue book and told us to get ready. After our tea was gone, the ritual began: we collected our three mugs and presented them to her. She examined them through her thick-rimmed black glasses, and then made sounds like oh or hmm or humph. Then, one by one, she would tell our fortunes, consulting her small book from time to time. "Your tea leaves are situated just so, look at that," she said, excited.

"What do they say?"

"Well, let's see here. They say that you will have a long life. A life filled with travels. Oh! Look at that, that small formation that looks like a triangle…That means you will get married and have lots of kids."

"Yuk!" I left the room, angry. Grandma wasn't fazed; she told me to watch television for a while, and angled her head at Laura's tea leaves.

Around bedtime, Grandma told us stories. They were always the same. "Your father was so gifted. He could read a map and decipher things like I've never seen anyone his age do. When he was just in elementary school he used to draw elaborate things…." She would eventually drift off, closing with some sentence about how our mother was his downfall. "Has she lost any weight yet?"

"Don't talk bad about Mom!" Laura demanded.

"Oh, I wouldn't dream to talk bad about your mother. She's a good cook. It's just I think you kids are spoiled. You don't know how to brush your hair. Look at you. She has you dressed like little boys with those clothes."

"We can't afford new clothes all the time, Grandma," I said.

"Well, neither can I, sweet, but I always manage to look nice. Come here and let me brush your hair." Grandma *was* immaculately dressed, though not in clothes I would have picked. She always wore a pressed, pale-colored blouse and tucked it into blue or black creased slacks. She was never without her hair curled and her face powdered, her high cheekbones accentuated with slightly too much rouge.

My hair was thick and curly, and puffed out like a cotton ball. When grandma brushed it, I had to stifle my crying because her comb would get caught in my curls. But to turn her down would be even more miserable. She cursed my hair as though it were talking back to her while she pulled and yanked my head around sharply. "Such pretty red hair, hmm…. You kids need to learn to take better care of yourselves."

Laura and I slept on Grandma's fold-out couch and sometimes awoke in the night to find her inspecting the contents of drawers or moving around the small porcelain figurines she collected. She seemed never to sleep. In the mornings, Grandma would be upbeat again, fixing us toast and jam or honey. Then, before Mom would pick us up, Grandma would tell us how disappointed she was in our behavior but how she would look forward to seeing us again, "if your mother ever allows you back." The way my parents had been arguing, I knew we'd be back soon enough.

***

Fashion magazines were a luxury that I would have to purchase with my own money, my parents said whenever I asked for a copy of *Vogue* or *Elle*, so when my mother took me to the store for the sole reason of buying me any three magazines I wanted, I knew something was up. We sat in the car with my haul, my mother smoking and looking straight ahead. Her hair was freshly highlighted with platinum streaks; I curled a piece around my finger. I could see she was nervous.

"We're getting divorced," she said.

"Finally," I said rudely, in my pre-teen way. When I noticed how genuinely sad she looked, I added, "I mean, it's good. You will be happier. You both will."

"We've discussed it, and I'll be the one moving out. It might take me a while to get on my feet." Not good, I thought. How could my father let her leave before she gets on her feet? By the time I left home, a few months later, I told myself that Mom had known what I had would come to realize, that the only way to win a fight with my father was to leave.

***

When Mom moved out, the tension at home hadn't dissipated, but, rather, solidified, making it tough for me—at the burgeoning and rebellious age of fifteen—to breathe. My father quickly became the target of all confusion, anger and rebellion my sister and I could muster. We became the target of his exhaustion and worry, his insistence on order during a time of chaos, his rigid regime. Between arguments, there were screaming fits, lengthy silences, and many punishments, resentments and rebellious moves. The argument that matters to this story, however, was the last one—the only one I remember with absolute clarity.

I had a date. My father, worn by his work day, was in the midst of his daily homecoming routine. He filled a mug with tap water and placed it in the microwave. As he rummaged around in the cabinets, I mustered up all the self-assurance I could.

I told Dad I was going to see my boyfriend, James. I had called Mom and she said it was okay. I was speaking as quickly as I could, explaining that James was expecting me.

"Ah-ha," he said. Then, turning toward me, setting a square tin of cocoa powder on the counter between us, he explained that it was too late to go out and meet anyone, especially a boy, no way in hell.

I repeated myself. "Mom said it was okay."

"Your mother isn't here to decide anything," he said.

After that, my memory of the conversation gets muddled and my voice becomes less reliable, more incensed. I began defending Mom's role as my parent, her voice in the matter of my freedom to go where I pleased. I didn't look at him as I made my case.

I continued to argue long enough to finish applying the pink polish, a task that made me look confident, unconcerned. I finished my pinky. I remember veering the argument away from Mom, insisting that I had spent a lot of time preparing for my date. I had flat-ironed my hair and applied dark eyeliner that I thought made my pale eyes look bigger. I was wearing vanilla-scented perfume and a silky black shirt. Did he think I was doing all this to have a Hot Pocket at home with him?

Dad stayed at the counter, arguing, also keeping with the completion of his task, stirring cocoa powder into a mug of hot water. His brown hair was long and straight and it hid his face whenever he lowered his head. The spoon clinked in his mug. I hated that sound. Each clink communicated the insignificance of what I was saying. I realized my arguments were getting nowhere, so I tried reasoning, then whining, then yelling. I strained my throat to drown out the sound of his clinking indifference.

My position ossified as my father stirred. I stood. *Clink.* I laced my arm through the strap of my purse. *Clink.* I took a few steps. Dad looked up.

"You're *not* going, and *that's* final," he snapped. Finally, some emotion.

"Watch me." I ran upstairs. Dad yelled after me, though he remained downstairs. We began yelling together, over each other's voices, both struck deaf and confident by our distance from each other. I didn't look at what I stuffed into my backpack; I just grabbed what I could from my closet and ran down the stairs, past him, beyond the living room, out the front door, around the wisteria bush, and into the alley that ran alongside our house.

Here I began taking steps backwards, away from the porch. I waited for Dad to come outside and admit he was wrong. Instead, when he appeared on the porch, he only watched. He wore a fresh pair of Asics, the whites of which disappeared as the alley stretched out between us. He was allowing me to go. I felt silly and dynamic at the same time. Each step I took tightened his gaze and reddened his skin. I turned.

"If you leave, don't come back," he yelled.

For years afterward my father and I would argue over what he said. I would say that he kicked me out by telling me not to come back. He would contend that I ran away and that he never said "Don't come back."

I still maintain that he said these words. However, it was obvious that I did run away, though at the time I had only planned to stay gone

one night. His words became my validation, my excuse for staying away for good.

I turned from my father. I lifted my head and walked toward the bus stop, thinking the whole thing was a divine intervention, that I had been given the opportunity to declare myself able, an adult. I reaffirmed my new reality with quickening strides. I looked back, still expecting Dad to have a change of heart, to chase me down the street. He shook his head and, to my surprise, walked back inside the house.

I walked toward the bus stop, clutching a backpack full of crumpled clothes. After I paid the fare and took a seat at the back of the bus, I uncurled my fingers. My bubblegum-pink nail polish was smeared across my palm. I was fifteen, old enough.

When I recall the day I left, the tension in my right hand is automatic, immediate. The images, on the other hand, come back to me in fragments and they always begin the same way: walking to the bus stop or staring out of the bus window, then time coiling inward in my mind, circling back to the beginning of the argument, trying to figure out how a simple argument got so out of control. What I do remember is what came next.

An Impressive Collection

James met me at the bus stop. It was at the end of his street, close to Buckeye Steel, a factory that employed most of the men in the neighborhood. I found relief in his smile. His arms were outstretched before I even got off the bus.

I hopped from the back door of the COTA and into his embrace. His solid white shirt smelled fresh and new and I was sure he bought it to look good for me. It hugged his slender, muscular body. He took my one bag—my life—in his hand and led me to my new home.

When I told James what had happened he didn't pause. "That settles it. You're moving in with me." He went on, explaining how excited he was to be "playing house" with me. He said he was getting older— nineteen—and thought he may be ready to settle down. I promised I wouldn't pressure him or overstay my welcome. He promised it wouldn't matter.

"You're just what I need," I told him.

"And you," he said, pulling me close as we walked, "are just what I want." He paused to examine my hand. "What the hell did you do to your fingernails?" James had a habit of critiquing my clothes and makeup and giving me vague suggestions about my hair.

I scratched at my nails and the dry polish on my palms. "Happen to have any nail polish remover?"

"Stop that. We can look. Dad's girlfriend leaves shit at our house all the time." He kissed me on the cheek, then the lips, then all over my cheeks in a sloppy display of affection. I felt happy to be with him, but I never liked the way he kissed, and I often wished we could skip that whole part of our relationship. But that was a small thing, I told myself then as my face air-dried.

***

I had met James at a teen center, a hangout that I used to frequent after school. The center was a nonprofit business that gave Short North kids a safe place to go and offered us certain opportunities, such as camping trips and art programs, which were designed to help us develop life skills. I was a regular, one of about twelve teenagers who showed up a few times a week and learned to dodge the more educational programs in lieu of a few pool games or some quality time lounging around with the other kids on the artfully-designed furniture that lined the walls of the backroom.

James had slipped in through the backdoor and began playing pool. A girl named Lee, whom I was smoking cigarettes with in the back of the club, sniggered. "That's him. That's that dude that beat up Damien. It was crazy, he started stripping off his clothes while he fought, he kept backing up a few steps then, rushing Damien again, he'd wail on him like this." She wailed on the empty space in front of her as the Newport that was dangling from her lips began to ash on her cleavage. I felt a pang of jealousy as I watched her breasts begin to peek out from her low-cut lacey tank. She continued to shadowbox, aiming uppercuts at an imaginary target and ducking when it hit back. When she stopped, she said, "Damien didn't get in one shot."

"Good. That fucker deserves it." I said this hoping Damien would walk in the door just then and take another beating that I could watch in real time.

"Yeah, I wish you were there. You would've loved it," she said.

Lee had dated Damien briefly, and it only took a week for her to start disappearing from the center for days at a time, rumors circulating that she had a black eye or fresh welt on her forehead. She never admitted to it, and that was typical, but we all knew he beat her. He beat every girl he was with.

I pointed at her cleavage. "You're brazenly exposed," I said, laughing. She rolled her eyes and stuffed her breast back below the lace while I turned to watch James. He was scrawny but muscular, and I noticed that he was sneaking glances in my direction. He sank a combination shot and then stood back and nodded at it. I admired his wide legged stance; it would have made him look tall if he hadn't been standing so close to Anthony, a friend of mine whose shoulder was level with the top of James's head. I was staring at him shamelessly, assessing: boxy ears, a stoner's heavy-lidded eyes, small nose, full lips. They weren't unattractive features, but they seemed mismatched somehow. "He's ugly," I concluded.

"Yeah, crazy, too," Lee said. "Come on, let's go. I'll introduce you."

***

I was quiet as we walked, consumed by each moment. The calm of evening had arrived and the light was just beginning to fade from a cloudless sky. James was talking incessantly about the neighborhood and who I would meet. This was my first trip to his house. James pointed to houses where his friends lived. I looked around, not speaking, just taking in the scene and nodding once in a while so he knew that I was listening.

The street was filled with fifties-era ranch homes, most of which were yellow or brown, spaced far enough apart that two homes could sit between each. We stopped at a brown house. It hunkered down on one side, as though it was sinking. James opened the door for me with just enough drama and grace to make a factory worker's shack seem like a mansion. The living room was sparse. There were two mustard-orange sofas that matched exactly in shape and length occupying two of the three walls, leaving the last one open except for an upside-down milk crate. A black and white television sat on the crate. I wasn't ready to go deeper into the house. I sat on a couch and leaned my head back against my hands. "Do you think I did the right thing? I mean, it's too late now, but...."

"Stop. I'll take care of you, okay? I promise," he said.

He cuddled against me. Originally, the plan was that I would meet him at his house and then we would walk to a diner a few blocks away, but time passed by and we never moved from the couch. We held each other and talked about our future. We were both interrupted by my stomach growling. James noticed the time and said that he had to get ready for work; he promised he would bring me home some food.

"Look around. This is your new home," he said and ran off to his room to get dressed. The living room led to a kitchen and then bathroom with standing shower only. I looked around the corner and found two other rooms at the end of a short hallway, both doors closed. I cracked the first door. Inside, I could see the outline of a man's body. His bloated stomach rose up and down, covered by a thin white sheet.

Next to the bed was the largest collection of porn videos I had ever seen. I could see mouths on cocks and painted red nails on bare flesh. There was a lot of teased blonde hair and large breasts with XXX and DIRTY written across them. I felt my face flush, but continued to stare. I had begun counting the number of tapes, so that I could later report the exact number to my friend Elisa, but James scared me from behind.

"Don't wake Dad."

I turned, whispering, "He has a lot of porn."

"Yeah, he's into that shit. Most of it's old, from the eighties. Listen, I work four hours tonight, but I got something in the fridge for you to sip on while I'm gone. A surprise."

"What should I do while you're gone?" I whispered.

"Watch TV or whatever." He puckered his lips for a kiss, which I turned away from, pretending not to notice. "Oh, and the reception is kind of bad, so you have to mess with the antenna to get it to work, especially on Channel 6."

"My house got Channel 4 and 6 and nothing else."

"Your old house," James said. "You're home now." He was walking away.

"Wait, um, does he know that I'm here?" I asked, nodding back to his father's room.

"Don't worry; he won't wake up until late. He works third shift." James smacked me on the butt and kissed my forehead, leaving a moist dot. He pushed away quickly, grabbing his purple Taco Bell visor and apron. He was late. From the window, I watched him run down the street. The yellow couch prickled against my knees. If he missed the bus, he would be at least twenty minutes late to work, which would mean his job. He couldn't afford to get fired again.

When he was gone, I sat on the couch, watching the phone. The house was completely quiet. I picked up the phone and dialed. The phone reception was fuzzy and I heard an occasional crumpling sound between rings. Jane, the friend Mom was staying with, answered.

"Hi, Jane. It's…." She interrupted me, thanking Jesus when she heard my voice.

"I am so glad you called, honey. You had us so worried. You know you can always come over here, sweetie, right?" she asked. I imagined her motioning for my mother in her pea green kitchen which, when I was younger and we would visit, was where she kept the phone and the ashtrays. Jane was my mother's other half. They were friends, but they seemed closer somehow, sharing a sort of familial bond, only with more understanding, more empathy. Jane and my mother would sit and smoke, drinking Pepsi and gossiping about mutual friends who were "in the program" while my sister and I watched cable in the other room. It was rare that we would be allowed to Jane's, and the cable was a treat. I actually considered Jane's offer that moment, but quickly dismissed it.

"Thanks, but I don't think that would work right now," I said carefully. "I really do appreciate it though." Jane didn't respond. There was a long pause before I heard a clunk as she set the phone down.

After a few seconds, I heard a rustling on the other end. "Mom?"

"Are you okay?" she asked in a muffled voice. The static made it seem as though we were worlds away. At the time, we were only a ten minute drive from the other, but as far as she knew I could have been anywhere.

"I am. I promise I'm okay. I needed to do this. But I want you to know that I ran away from Dad, not you," I said. "You know that, right?"

She was quiet.

"Look, Mom, I'm just sick of it. He tries to fix me. He tries to control everything I do. I just want to live my own life, and he's gotten worse since you've been gone."

"Your father loves you," she said. This was the last thing I wanted to hear. Battling the creeping sensation of guilt, I began to pace, staring down at the hardwood floor. A few incense sticks stood up from cracks in the ground, some burnt to the nub. I bent to light one and tried to rephrase.

"Mom, look, I don't want Dad to find me." As I blew on the flame a sparse smoke released a familiar spicy, honey-laced scent that James often had in his hair. "I don't want him to give you a hard time, and I know this wasn't the best way to...Look, I'm just going to stay where I am for a while. I just want you to know that I'm safe and sound. I'm okay." I heard Mom's jagged breath, and I realized she was crying. "I love you, Mom, okay?"

"Your father is worried, too. It won't be any problem for me," she began. She sounded as though she were underwater now, and I could picture the salty tears. My stomach grew hot as I reasoned that her tears were not my fault at all. I began to feel the prickliness of my argument with Dad well up again, consuming my thoughts.

"The truth is that Dad told me not to come back," I said. I heard a shift in her breath, as though she were considering what to say next. "So," I went on, "I don't have a choice. I'm sorry if I hurt you, and I'll call you tomorrow. Love you, Mom." I hung up the phone hastily.

I turned on the TV to an episode of *Growing Pains*. The picture waved and I began to fiddle with the antenna, thinking I could postpone reality a bit longer, when I heard a scratching sound in the kitchen. I followed the noise to a side door where a small striped cat pawed at an empty metal bowl. I went to grab some milk from the refrigerator and noticed a plastic bag with a note that had my name scrawled on it. Inside were two bottles of flavored malt liquor. It was my "surprise." I grabbed both. I poured the cat some milk and sat next to him as I unscrewed one of the bottles. Together, we drank on the stoop. The berry flavored malt liquor was fizzing down my throat in gulps. The next one would taste better, slightly warmed.

I stroked the cat and stared longingly at the house next door. It didn't appear that anyone lived there. It was painted white and the grass behind it reached the windows. Dad used to let our backyard grow like that; we called it the jungle. I walked up to the house and peeked inside. The walls were marked with large black splotches, maybe from a fire. The carpet was pulled up at one corner revealing an uneven wooden floor. I tried to open a window, but it was stuck. This was where I really wanted to live, completely alone. I would fix it up and invite others into my world only on my own terms.

By the time I was on my second twenty-two ounce brew my head felt light and the cat was long gone. I had decided Dad needed a while to cool off, but I would go home in a few weeks. In the meantime, I needed a job. If I had a car, I could find a good job; the decent-paying positions were always in the suburbs, nowhere near downtown, unless I could get a job at one of the banks. With the thought of finding a job, I realized that I now relied on James for food and shelter. With the thought of food, my stomach roared.

I hadn't eaten anything all day. I explored the compartments of a near-empty refrigerator once, twice, three times. There was nothing to be had. Maybe James would remember to bring back some burritos. The adrenaline from the day must have caught up with me because I felt drained. I went back and watched the wavy black and white television from the hard floor, finding it more comfortable than the yellow couch. I was sipping my brew as though it was tea now, trying to reconnect with *Days of Our Lives*, a soap that my Grandma used to say I should watch because I shared one of the character's names. I sat close to the TV, with the sound low. I must have been in some sort of a trance because I didn't even hear him approach me.

"There's an, um, g-g-girl in my house."

I looked up to see James's father standing over me in a tight white shirt and briefs. To my relief there was nothing intimidating about him. His legs were small and dark, as hairless as my own. He was scratching his balding head. "We've met once before, sir," I said with a huge fake smile, extending my hand. "At the bus stop." He took it with his left hand and squeezed.

"I-I-I-I know, I remember your pretty little self. Little Red," he said, walking off, looking in the empty refrigerator. He shuffled around a bit and I followed him into the kitchen where I sat at the table, to make small talk. "You know how to cook?" he asked.

"Not really, but I could try. I know how to make some pretty good quickie meals, like I used to add Italian spices to that frozen ravioli they sell at Kroger's and then use a mixture of white sauce and marinara. I could make that for you one day. I also know how to make cookies and all kinds of deserts. I can make any kind of cookie you like; I used to help my mom with Christmas cookies and we'd make hundreds of them to give to her friends." I would have gone on, but the illegitimacy of my own childlike listing of meals was irritating even me.

"That sounds good, kid," he said. He was still rummaging around as I sat, hyper-aware, in the tall wooden chair. He stomped, startling me. "Fuck! Who drank all the milk?"

"Oh, sorry, that was me. I'll go buy some more if you want."

He scratched his head. "You know where the nearest store is? It's a mile away, over the bridge that way. Next time buy the new milk before you drink it all. I'm not mad at you, though. No, I'm not mad. Everyone makes mistakes. I'm not mad at all." He was outlining the rules of his house, I thought.

"I understand, Mr. Emer. I really am sorry."

Although he said it was okay and that he forgave me, I noticed that when he spoke to me it was almost as though he was speaking to himself. He welcomed me to the house, but explained that I could only stay there for a while because his girlfriend might move back in soon. They might be getting married, but I shouldn't tell anyone about that because they might get jealous. He patted me on the back, an innocuous, father-like gesture and said that I could make up for my error by baking him some peanut butter cookies one day. Then, he disappeared into his room and I heard his television come on through the walls—a game show. It sounded as though his TV was in better shape than the one in the living room. I was betting it even had color. This might not be so bad, I thought. I'll have to buy my own milk.

***

I was famished by the time James got back. I sat on his porch in anticipation as he ran back to me the same way he ran away. It was dark outside, but I could see he held a large white bag with grease stains on the bottom. I ate four burritos that day and his dad ate the rest. The three of us drank beer until the sun went down, burning sticks of incense in between cigarettes out on the porch. Mr. Emer insisted that the air smell nice, even if we were outside. He also insisted that we take off our shoes in the house, which he never cleaned. Sometimes he asked us to show him what was in our jacket pockets, so that he knew we weren't stealing from him.

I sat on that porch smoking, happy. Neighbors walked by and I received more than one extended glance because I didn't know many of James's friends; I was the new girl. James had a reputation because he was arrogant, outgoing. His friends had often commented that we were mismatched; I was too reserved to keep up with him. I would shrug, say that we balanced each other out. Meanwhile, I coveted his sense of place in the world, his confidence and energy. I still hadn't found anything that interested me enough to become, or to maintain his level of excitement about simple things, like a big meal, a long walk to a friend's house to smoke weed, a good song, sex, even fighting, arguing, starting trouble just to see what happened. All of it bored me, or scared me. I enjoyed one thing then, one thing that proved far easier at James's home: getting drunk.

I thought maybe I could learn from James, absorb a bit of his vigor, and I asked him to show me how to appreciate things more. He said it began with reputation. Once other people knew you, respected you, he said, you can do whatever you want and get away with it. He told me that when he started a fight with someone for looking at him wrong at a bar or for standing too close to his house, it was because he was only 5'6" and he had to prove himself in the neighborhood. He said his father taught him how to fight and talk loud in order to gain respect.

Sometimes his big mouth would embarrass me, like when we were at the grocery store or the mall and he would tell the sales clerk that he deserved some additional discount because he had to wait so long in line. If anyone gave him a hard time, he would ask to speak to a manager, loud, but never irate. It was all a scam. He would sometimes steal something right off the shelf and walk up to the cash register, saying he wanted to return it. To my surprise, this scam often worked, but I always worried that we would both go to jail.

James introduced me around the neighborhood. It seemed like everyone respected him, offering him beer or a hit of weed to hang for a while, inviting him over for movies or to watch a basketball game. I often sat in rooms filled with smoke, passing on a blunt. I had smoked once or twice and felt socially impeded by the stuff. Everything I looked at seemed either comical or threatening. So, I passed. I was teased for being a lightweight.

James and his friends often talked about money, during commercial breaks. They spoke of investing the amounts they all worked shitty jobs for. Investing meant buying and selling weed or crack, "flipping" was the common term. Crack was for the hotshots, the men that carried guns and used them; James wasn't that sort, though he talked as though he was. James only talked. I still believe he was a decent person, someone born and led into a series of unfortunate places. Too bad for him, he was intelligent. Too bad for me, he didn't care.

He only confided in me later that he was no good at selling weed because he would smoke it all, and that he didn't like the idea of selling crack because he didn't have a place to stash it; he worried that his father's girlfriend might get to it. She was a thief, an addict, he said. "Wait until you meet her."

The one thing James did talk about was joining the Bloods; the south side of Columbus was full of them. Where I was from it was all Crips and Folks, gangs that wore blue and black. Here it was red. Bandanas peeking from baggy jeans meant power; these bandanas also meant that those who wore them might get shot or beaten. James told me who was already "in". I asked him why it was taking him so long to join and he laughed. He said he didn't like the induction, that you have to get beaten by at least five guys and he never did like to take a punch.

"It's not like I can't fight," he assured me. "Dad taught me to be quick." He demonstrated, ducking an imaginary punch and then jabbing at the air. I thought his relationship with his father was sweet. "You know that boy that used to mess with you at school is a Folk. I should beat his ass." He was talking about Damien, who used to follow me home and slap me on the butt or in the back of the head. One day, not too long before I left home, he had followed me from the bus stop. Just before making it to my front porch he pushed me to the ground, stealing my Walkman and then kissing me on the cheek before running off. It had been my last day at high school.

"I'm over it, James. I'm never going back to school anyway. Besides, I don't want you to join. Everyone around here likes you anyway, so who cares if you're 'in' or not? Just keep being cool, get a better job."

"We'll see," he said. "This is where I grew up, but sometimes the connections are better if you move out of the neighborhood. You know I want to get us out of Dad's house soon, right? I'm saving up." Later that day, James bought a forty dollar bag of weed from a man who lived at the end of the street. We wouldn't be moving out together anytime soon.

We sat out on the stoop and I asked James about the abandoned house in front of us while he smoked.

"That house has been empty for a while now. No one's staying around here. See that house down there, the green one? That's empty, too, and the other darker green one, that one, too. People are moving out because the factory's firing people. My Dad's lucky he still has a job."

"This neighborhood does seem to be dying," I said. I lit a cigarette. "Where do you want to move?"

"I'm south side for life, you know that. I'm thinking somewhere around Parsons or South High Street. I need to find a better job, construction or something. This Taco Bell shit isn't adding up fast enough."

"I need to find work, too," I said. I resolved to take the bus downtown the next day and find a job.

***

Our bedroom was dark when we closed the door. A blanket covered the window. We often had awkward sex in the morning. James moving while I remained still; I made noises that I thought were appropriate. I didn't really enjoy sex, but I knew it was what people did, so I did it. James was my first and I was still learning. Maybe I would grow to like it? I liked James.

He approached me a second time one morning. We were on the bed and I was face down. I remember hearing a door, feeling a quick jerk, and silencing my faux-moan. James pulled out and ran to the door. He shut it and lay back down, lit a cigarette and passed it to me. Apparently, we were done for the morning. I took a deep puff, and was about to ask what was wrong when I heard the floor creak outside the door. I heard another door open and shut. James kissed me on the forehead and took the cigarette, and smashed it in the ashtray by the bed. That kiss on the forehead was the part I liked about sex with James. He always held me, and kissed me there tenderly after. That morning, we fell back asleep in each other's arms.

***

I found a part-time job at Bob Evans where I cleared dirty dishes off of tables and occasionally took drink orders when we were busy. The manager promised me a serving position when I turned sixteen. I knew that servers made good money, so I worked hard, trying to prove myself. I was squirreling away money and the rest went under James's bed, for a down payment on a new place. James tried to contribute as well, but he could barely keep his job at Taco Bell; he regularly got sent home early. We would fight about this. Meanwhile, I was mostly angry because it felt good to be away from him sometimes. I thought about getting a place of my own instead, starting over again.

I lived with James and his father for a few months, saving money and contributing the occasional groceries before I began to feel that my time there was coming to an end. My stomach hurt from the nightly Taco Bell, and James's father had begun blaming me every time there was something missing from the fridge. Apparently not all was forgiven from the day one milk incident. I had also met Sheila, who turned out to be a geeker (crack head) who routinely fucked, stole, and fled from James's dad. I had only seen her in passing, but she reminded me of the women on Mr. Emer's outdated porn tapes. Despite her erratic behavior, Mr. Emer was in love and he chose to blame his son for "keeping her away," when she didn't show up for a while.

"It's not me, Dad. Don't you get it? Crack rock drives her off. She's a goddamn crack head." This would begin a yelling match that came to blows occasionally. It always ended with James taking my hand and pulling me out the door, his dad yelling about the gun he kept in his bedroom. We would stay the night down the street at Mrs. Carlile's house. She was a plump woman who kept her long hair in a white-streaked bun. She fed us cereal and rolled her eyes each time I spoke.

I hadn't ever considered going back home, not since the day I had left. Not even the night Mr. Emer tried to kiss me. I had been off that day and had spent most of the day watching TV while Mr. Emer slept. After watching a series of rerun sitcoms, I decided to go to the corner store across the bridge. Before leaving, I thought I'd see if Mr. Emer was awake, to see if he wanted anything. Quietly, I approached his bedroom door and found it cracked, as usual. When I saw that he was sitting up straight, watching what sounded like Jerry Springer, I knocked lightly. "Come in," he sang.

"Sorry to bother you, Sir. I just wanted to know whether you wanted anything from the store. I'm about to leave right now."

"Sweet girl. Good girl to ask me that," he said. His tone was soft and it crept through the room, crawled up my legs as I took steps back, through the doorway and reached for a piece of paper that from the dividing window to the kitchen.

"I can pick up some Ramen noodles," I offered. Surprising me, he stood and walked toward me, wearing only a V-neck white T-shirt and briefs. I walked into the kitchen, pretending to look for a pen. "I can't find anything to write with, but I can probably remember," I said.

"I don't want anything from the store, I don't think." He turned from me and opened a cabinet, inspecting it briefly.

"Okay. I'll be back soon, then," I said.

"Wait a minute. Let me check the fridge," he said quickly, still with a soft creepiness that had now snuck into my chest, causing my heart rate to quicken. After opening and closing the freezer door, he turned to me. "You know what I need?" He stepped to me, seeming to invite me to flee. Something in his stance made me think that if I dodged him, he'd be ready. The fading lightning bolt tattoo on his calf caught my attention as he stood, edging in closer to me.

"No," I said.

"You like my tattoo? I was a runner."

"Me, too," I said, hoping we could change the tone here, talk about road races.

"I was fast," he said.

"Um, I ran distance."

"You weren't fast?" I could taste his breath as he pushed me up against the wall, his eyes spotted with broken blood vessels. I realized that he was speaking without stuttering, and as I inhaled his breath, I felt as though we were tucked together in the deep recesses of a drawer. I frantically pushed him away and rushed to the front room. Instead of chasing, he began to stutter again. He was offering an apology in his normal, deep tone, stating that he thought I was Sheila for a minute and got carried away in his emotions. I told him it was okay and asked if I could wait on his couch. There wasn't a bus coming for almost an hour and I had decided to go to Kroger's instead of the corner store. He said sure and disappeared into his bedroom, looking distressed. Some long minutes later he reemerged with an empty wine bottle, a sharp tone that reminded me of the day I had moved in, three months earlier. "You drink my liquor?"

"No, Sir." I stood up, rigid as a soldier, reading to run. I was stupid to stick around after that strange episode. What the fuck had I been doing, just sitting there on the couch, stewing in what had happened while I was still in this man's house?

"James! James drank my bottle of fine liquor."

"I don't think so, sir."

"Y-y-you always stick up for him. You love him? Y-you love my son?"

"I have love for your son, yes sir."

"Come here, then, if you love my son." I took a step toward him and then retreated. Mr. Emer grabbed the back of my hand and assured that this would only take a minute. I could still go to the store, but he wanted to show me something important. He led me to his room and pointed to a collection of dusty liquor and wine bottles he kept in rows against his wall, behind a nightstand. I found myself back in the doorway as he showed me all the places where he marked his bottles with thick inky lines. And then he held them up to the light, showing me that the alcohol was lower than these lines. He sloshed them around so that I couldn't tell if they actually contained less liquid than marked. "I know you like to drink," he stated. I noticed his speech was disturbingly smooth again and I walked out. "You want some?" he called out.

"No, thank you, Sir." I turned to leave and he responded by rushing toward me. He examined my eyes, not looking into them as much as at them, then my face as a whole. I looked back, watching him watch me.

"I want some of you," he said lowly, beneath raised eyebrows; he was an inch from my face. He cupped my tiny breast in his hand. I should have screamed or punched him, but instead I was quiet, docile. His other hand slid behind me, stopping on my butt. He held me like this in the doorway for a moment and I responded with a cold stare. Then, he kissed me full on the lips as though to say "gotcha." I continued to stare, no longer struck by fear but anger. I could feel the heat of it building in my throat and I searched for something to strike him with. It was here, with his hands on me, that I decided Mr. Emer wasn't high. He was insane. I didn't believe he knew who I was; this was a different man. There was no sound between us but the low-level buzzing sound coming from his television.

Now, through the doorway of his room, I could make out the screen. A man wore a cowboy hat and beat a woman with a whip. The anger spread to my arms, to my hands, which clenched tightly as Mr. Emer held me there. I was frozen, unable to decide how to break this embrace when he caught me off guard. "I've seen you," he said. His voice got lower, his face closer to mine. "It's the only reason I let that little bastard stay here for free."

With this comment, a strange stoicism washed over me, dissipating the anger. I pushed him off him with all my force. I turned on my heel and walked away at a normal pace. If he chased me, I'd fight. I'd claw and kick and bite. Somehow, I knew he wouldn't chase me. I went out of the house, down the street, and waited for the bus. I have a job, I thought, I don't have to put up with this. It wasn't until I had been sitting at the bus stop a few minutes that I began to shake.

I had lived with James and his father from August until the middle of November. It was almost Thanksgiving. Every day, I rode the COTA down High Street, past a small restaurant that Dad and I used to go to. At the front entrance, Dad's stained-glass panels had replaced the tiny windows that used to be there. I appreciated them. They were simple designs, expertly done. I thought about how I always watched Dad sketch out his designs. He had been working on a series of new sketches when I left.

Because it was Sunday, I knew Dad and Laura would be at Grandma's house for dinner. I stopped the bus by my old home. I tried the front door and jiggled the key, but it wouldn't go in. I went around to the back. Everything was quiet in the neighborhood, and even the few homeless men who still sometimes huddled around our garage in the winter weren't there.

Dad had thought to change the locks, but did he remember that he had also shown Laura and me how to break in? I opened a ground level window with a piece of thin sheet metal that was stashed around the back of the house and looked around before scooting up to the window and edging myself in. I fell hard on the basement floor and replaced the window, locking it back into place.

When I rushed upstairs, I was ambushed by Honey, our Cocker Spaniel. I kneeled down to hug her and she began jumping around, too excited to stay still. She hadn't barked when I broke in, I thought. To her, this was still my home. I gave Honey a piece of American cheese from the fridge and took a few slices of thinly-sliced turkey, laying them on my tongue appreciatively. I threw a piece to Honey and told her I wanted to stay. Then, I began to look around. The house was immaculate and this seemed foreign to me. I was used to at least a little mess, a light coating of Honey's hair on the living room carpet. The sterility was what reminded me that I was only here to get a few things.

I ran upstairs, grabbed some clean clothes and some other miscellaneous things from my room, and wrote a note.

> *In case you're wondering, I'm OK. Have a happy Thanksgiving.*
> *Your Daughter*

I picked up the phone and dialed James at work.

"Your father yelled at me and I left," I told him, and said I'd fill him in later, when I was settled somewhere. I thanked him for letting me stay there and save some money.

"I have a lot of love for you, girl," he said. "Dad didn't get too crazy, did he?" Before I could answer, he yelled to someone that he was coming then told me to call him tomorrow. He would be out tonight on a run, he said quietly, and it was a good thing I wouldn't be there because he wasn't planning on going home until late. "I'm coming up on some good shit, an ounce at least," he said, as though he'd actually sell this new stash of weed, not just smoke it. I told him not to inhale. We both laughed, and then he excused himself; there was a fat lady waiting for her burritos, he said.

As I stood in my father's living room, I knew this would never again be my home. Dad's words would repeat themselves, magnifying meaning and becoming a renewable excuse, keeping me away. They had somehow soaked into the brick walls of this house on Mount Pleasant. My hand traced the wall, everything solid and boldly outlined like a cartoon. This was *my* story, no longer shared with my family, but all mine; and I couldn't go backwards in it. I would not return with a bowed head. Besides, even if I had wanted to, how could I face him? What would I say?

I can still remember what it was like to sit on that COTA bus, peering out the window, thinking the worst was over, the world was still mine for the taking. I had to leave everything and everyone behind, even those who cared about me. I *had* to. I can still relate to that sense of longing, that tiny feeling in the depth of my stomach that egged me on. I had to keep moving.

Miss Sarah

I have concluded that if some sort of genetic destiny *had* propelled me to run away to live with James, it was pushing me again, as I hopped off the COTA bus on the north side of Columbus. The bus ride from my father's house was easier the second time. I had been locked out, and I no longer felt as though I was making the decision to run. Rather, I was doing what I had to do. I remember getting off the bus on the north side of town, pausing at a pay phone. I decided I could tell from my father's voice whether he had read my note yet. As I stood there, my quarter poised, I decided to call him later. I strode toward Elisa's house; my best friend would be there for me, I thought. She would know what to do next.

Elisa's mother, Miss Sarah, had extended an open invitation to me. "Your crazy-ass father has gone too far this time. I understand. If you want to stay with us a while, you are more than welcome! Just bring yourself on over." She had no idea of what went on in my father's house, but her uninformed mercy was a blessing. I heard her words over and over, resounding in my head while I walked and they provided something just short of a hop in my step. I had been convincing myself that I would be received well. I was in the suburbs now. I stood shaking on her porch, crisp suburban air cutting through me.

Miss Sarah opened her arms when she saw me. "I know this is a hard time for you, Red. Come in, we'll help you out." I hugged her a little too tightly and dropped my bag full of dirty clothes among the paperwork and makeup samples strewn about her front room. I was already familiar with this house. I had spent many nights here. I hadn't told Elisa I was coming yet, so I couldn't wait to break the news to her. "We're like sisters now," I imagined I would say, and we would spend all night talking and doing our hair in styles we saw in magazines.

Miss Sarah told me all she had heard about Dad's home since I left.

"I heard that your sister is pretty upset."

I nodded.

"I heard that she locked herself in a closet until your Dad agreed to give her twenty dollars for a movie."

"Really?" I had heard little of what went on at Mount Pleasant since I left. All I knew came from brief conversations with Mom. My sister and Elisa's brother were best friends, so Miss Sarah was probably getting her information from him. It was possible that she was talking to Mom, too. They had been friends until Miss Sarah began trying to push her makeup line on my mother. When I told Mom I would be living with Elisa, she was relieved. Mom was moving into a small apartment a few blocks from Dad now. We were only able to speak every few days, but we connected to confirm that we were both okay. The divorce was still hovering over everything, and what I did not know at the time is that she and Miss Sarah had conspired to offer me a warm place to stay. If I stayed on good behavior, Miss Sarah had agreed to accept me into her home until I came to my senses and could move in with Mom. My reasons for not living with my mother right away were, one, my father would show up at her apartment and blame her for my refusal to come back, and that would lead to more fighting; two, she was struggling with money. The last thing she needed was to worry about me.

Miss Sarah plopped two large, callous-heeled feet on the glass coffee table. I sat across from it and stretched. My feet ached in my worn tennis shoes. There was silence and I realized I was being rude. "You look good," I said. "Are you losing weight?" I said this to break the silence, knowing Miss Sarah was always on a diet or soon to begin a new one.

"Thank you," she said as she reached for a bag of rice cakes. She pushed half a cake into her mouth and then replaced the bag on the table alongside another, empty package.

When Miss Sarah asked me what happened and why I left, I shrugged because I wanted to appease her and I was unsure what she wanted to hear. "Dad and I just don't get along anymore." She asked me for specifics. I think she wanted to hear that he brutalized me, verbally degraded me, something …but I just shrugged again. "I don't want to talk about it."

She shrugged as well, probably figuring that my wounds were still too fresh. So she changed the subject to business. She often told me that Mary Kay was more than a simple career for housewives; it was an opportunity to grow as a businesswoman. And, if you took it seriously enough, it was a lifestyle. She said it was the sort of lifestyle I could benefit from. She had welcomed me into this lifestyle. Another open invitation, wide open.

"Can I have a rice cake?"

She kept her eyes on me, narrowed, and a smile spread across her face. She was settling into some thought, probably one of pride for rescuing me. "This is my last one," she said, handing it to me. "I guess since you're my red-headed step-child now, you can have it."

I ran upstairs with my rice cake half eaten, and made room to sit on the floor by the window by pushing Elisa's pile of clothes into more defined mounds by the walls. I stared outside a while, looked through Elisa's make up, and then settled in on her bed. I didn't intend to fall asleep, but the comfort of this house was nice. It had all the welcoming of my father's house, without the judgment. I slept better than I had during the entire time I stayed with James.

***

Elisa and I had been friends since we were ten, or maybe nine; I don't remember. What I do remember is watching from my porch as a van pulled up to the yellow house down the street. I watched her and her brother stand outside with her family as moving trucks arrived. They all stood out there watching as large men in open-fingered gloves pulled their possessions out of the truck and pushed them into the house. I wondered why they didn't help. It seemed quite lazy to me. Dad would have made us move the boxes, I remember thinking, and rightfully so. Who were these people that they had money to waste on such trivial things?

I wondered if they knew that the yellow house they were so extravagantly moving into was close to a crack house. People didn't stay in that house long. I watched Elisa, who was my age, but looked far older than her ten years; she was plump, and as she stood outside talking with a large, toothy smile I noted that she had an incredibly pretty face. Her skin was the tone I longed for, buttermilk honey, smooth. Her eyes were large, even without eyeliner. I decided right then and there that I had no desire to meet her.

My parents began noticing my preference to stay at home, and they determined that I was a recluse. "Maybe she just needs a little help making friends," I heard Mom explain to Dad.

"She's a bit introverted," Dad said.

A week later, my sister had become close to Mike, Elisa's brother, who was my sister's age. Mom said it was time that I meet Elisa. I refused. I recall growing quite crafty in order to avoid meeting new people. Kids, especially, were threatening to me, dangerous. I preferred TV to playing outside where one could fall and crack open her head. Moreover, characters in books, in movies, in stories, were far more interesting and far more attractive to me than other kids. Real life, real kids were all so careless, so quick to tease or laugh when I said the wrong thing.

Two weeks later, Laura announced that Mike's cat was giving birth. Mom, never one to miss an opportunity to coax me away from my room, saw this as an opportunity. "Jen, how would you like a new kitten?" Later, my mother would regret this decision when the cat I picked would run away, pad home a day or so later, happy, hungry, pregnant. Ultimately, the cat would repeat this trend numerous times and give birth to around twenty kittens over the course of five litters. Mom would wrap up the small, shaky newborns in hand towels and bounce them like babies, asking me who was going to take these ones and why I had raised my cat to be such a whore.

Mom sent me over to Elisa's house. My excitement overwhelmed any desire I had to stay at home, to avoid contact with the new neighbors. "I'm here to pick out a kitten," I said proudly to Mike's mom, who smiled widely as she looked down at my short, red-headed self. I looked up at her, my hexagon-shaped glasses pushing against my face, as they did when I looked up, and waited for her to stop smiling and show me to the kittens, so I could get back home.

"You must be Laura's sister, right? Laura and Mike are playing in the backyard!"

"Uh-huh," I said absently.

"Come on in."

Miss Sarah wore pale pink curlers in her hair. She smiled and spoke in a voice that almost seemed to sing. As she waved me deeper into the house, I was unsure which way to go—the place was bloated with junk and there were big piles of clothes in the corner of the front room and open boxes all over the place. Open packages of cookies and Doritos were strewn on the counters and I stepped over half-eaten plates of food that were left in front of the television. I was ready to walk out when I noticed that their television was bigger than I'd seen. *Okay*, I thought, *I'll give it a chance*.

"Just go up the stairs and make a left. My daughter loves to meet new people," she said. *I don't want to make a friend*, I thought, but I *did* want to see kitties.

When I knocked on the door to Elisa's room, it creaked and swung open. It was like walking into a toy store. Her room was crammed with games and clothes piles, just like those downstairs. She was listening to music and playing with three little yellowish-orange fuzz balls. *The kitties!!!* I ran over to them.

"Who are you?" she asked, rudely.

"I live down the street."

"Oh, that's right, Laura's sister!" A moment of silence passed before she turned to me, hands on hips, "I'm Elisa. What do you want to be?"

The question was a strange icebreaker. "You mean when I grow up?"

"Yeah, I am going to be a doctor. I'll get my Ph.D. from Harvard and then I'll be a female doctor!" The way she said it, I could tell it was rehearsed. I wondered what a Ph.D. was.

I thought about saying I wanted to be a biker, but I was yet to learn how to ride a bike. "I want to be a gypsy," I said, just as firmly as she had.

She laughed at me. "You're weird."

"I think I'll name her Apricat," I said, reaching for the smallest orange kitten I could find.

"No. That one's mine!" Elisa said.

"I thought you already had a cat."

"Well, I want two."

"Fine," I said, "I'm leaving." No cat.

Elisa and her mother showed up at my house later that day. Elisa glared at me with toffee-colored eyes. Apricat meowed weakly in her thick arms. She gave me a half-hearted apology. Then she winced. Her mother had a tight grip on her hand. "Do you want to play or something?" Her lips were tight. The kitten began to purr as soon as I petted her fluffy orange back. She burrowed her face into my arm.

***

A few years later we cried together on my porch after Elisa's family announced their plans to move to the suburbs. Their home on our street had been broken into by three teenagers with black scarves covering their mouths. Our neighborhood had made the news quite a few times for its staggering crime rate, and Elisa's father said he wouldn't put his family in danger any longer.

Reports spoke more and more of a gang known as the Short North Posse, a destructive force in the neighborhood that bordered our street. The Columbus Police had waged war against the gang, and every night the news reported on plans to clean up the neighborhood. Reporters said that the Short North would soon be revitalized and crime-free. Meanwhile, boys my age were the ones being initiated and trained to continue the reign, if only by some other name.

I had to admit, Elisa's new home *was* enviable. A satellite dish sat on the roof, and she had a television of her very own in her room. She also had her own phone. I suddenly realized why we never spent the night at my house. Late at night, in her basement, I enjoyed watching shows I would otherwise never see, so I accepted the lopsided relationship we had. Miss Sarah often commented about my family's strangeness (excluding me), and I would agree, pleased to receive some sympathy. She had a minor friendship with my mom and whenever more than a few weeks passed without some kind of contact between them, Miss Sarah pressed me for details about my parents' interactions.

After her parents went to bed, Elisa and I would sneak little tastes of her father's gin and smoke Benson & Hedges cigarettes that we had stolen from Mom's purse. I put my mouth to Elisa's window and blew out the smoke. "I want a boyfriend," I said, looking down her street at a row of identical houses. It had been over a month since Elisa had set foot in my house.

"Well, you don't really need one, but you should at least kiss a boy. Look, this quiz says that most girls have been kissed by the time they are thirteen. We're already thirteen. We're late!" She paused. "I don't even think I know a boy who wants to kiss me. It's probably because I'm fat."

"Boys make fun of my glasses," I offered, hoping to make her feel better. It didn't seem to work, so I added, "Besides, they like fat girls. Fat girls have bigger boobs." This made her cry.

We read those magazines voraciously, picking out our flaws and comparing them to the airbrushed perfection of the magazine pages. They told us to be tall, skinny, and acne-free. Even the articles on self-esteem would feature some cartoon-perfect girl pouting in a chair, and we would wonder what the fuck she had to be so sad about. It was as though you needed to be perfect in order for your suffering to matter. Elisa and I grew to depend on each other's misery to validate our own.

After years of pretending to be sisters, wishing we were, we lived together.

"So you're staying in my room?" Elisa woke me with a shake.

"Huh? Uh, yeah," I said, "we're roomies! Won't it be fun?"

She looked unconvinced; this was not the elation I expected, now that we were sisters. She looked at me as though I was complete violation of her personal space, and she would now have to display dominance. This was the way of sisters. Had I really forgotten that?

"You'll have to sleep over there. I don't have two beds." She pointed below the window. Then she laughed and gently punched me in the arm. "Just kidding. Look at your face!" I didn't laugh. I was exhausted, desperate, and she knew it. Her voice softened, "Mom wants you to go to the Mary Kay meeting with us tonight." She sighed, smoothing her hair in place as she angled a handheld mirror around her ponytail. "Please come. It will be more fun with you there."

When we arrived, the Mary Kay meeting seemed like the place to be. It was a genuine party, although the number of old women there made it pretty lame. There was plenty to eat—mostly desserts. Activities were outlined in a pamphlet that promised door prizes and free makeovers. There were tables full of Mary Kay makeup that we could sample. I signed up for a makeover, and climbed up into a chair surrounded by women. Delighted, a squat woman with teased hair hovered over me, examining my skin. "We have to cover up those pesky freckles," she said. I rolled my eyes and asked Miss Sarah if she could do my makeover. I didn't realize that Miss Sarah would slather my lips with tangerine gloss and my eyelids with orange eye shadow. I looked over at Elisa whose perfectly smooth skin was being accented by subtle browns and taupe. I was jealous. I suggested more neutral tones. Miss Sarah explained this would wash me out.

"Trust me, girl, I'm a professional."

The woman bent over me and began to cover my face in layer upon layer of foundation. I could smell garlic on her breath. The foundation felt thick and heavy, even sticky as it adhered to my skin. I closed and opened my eyes, as directed, and after an excruciatingly long time, she was done. When presented with a mirror, I saw that I looked as I felt; I was wearing a mask. It wasn't as bad as I had suspected, and I began to consider buying some of the stuff that she'd shellacked me with. No one would ever have to know what I really looked like, or that I had easily-irritated skin. The woman with the teased hair took my picture with a Polaroid, then one of Elisa and laid them on the table among others. Each picture would be entered in a contest for best makeover, "and the winner will win a lipstick" an animated voice said. Elisa would win. She said she always did, and when we returned home later, she would show me her collection of lipsticks, generously offering me pick from the softer shades.

After assessing our pictures, Elisa nudged me. "We should try and sneak out for a cigarette." I agreed fully, but as we stood, a woman in a long skirt and dotted-pink cheeks stopped us with an ear-splitting, southern-dipped holler. "Well, don't you two go anywhere, now, we're really going to get going'. 'Isn't that right ladies?"

A succession of tapping filled the room, sharp plastic tapping and gritty wood tapping. The sound filled the room and hung there in the air like a heavy cloud. Each woman was armed with a clapper that she continued to work until I felt the sharp pang of a headache; these women seemed empowered by this irritating sound. Elisa mouthed something I couldn't understand.

"What?" I said, somewhat louder than intended. A woman darted her head around, her long neck twisting like a coiled snake. I had interrupted the Sunday gospel. I straightened my back, stilled my face, and waited for her to turn away as her eyes remained fixed on me. I turned to Elisa, nudging her back.

"*What*?" I mouthed.

Her lips moved: "I—was wrong! This isn't fun no way, not even with you here!" Then she lifted two fingers to her mouth. I felt the outline of a pack of Newports in my pocket, and my knee began to bounce. I watched as the Mary Kay guru as she began to preach about Christianity. "God comes first in your lives, ladies, then family, then business. That's the way of life here. That's how we remain centered. That's how we achieve success." The room was quiet, filled with nodding heads. I felt that there was a vague similarity between these meetings and the one I had attended with Mom. There it had been recovery before family, but the Mary Kay lifestyle seemed no less rigorous despite this fact. Miss Sarah had moved to the front row and taken a seat, completely engaged in this woman's speech.

People began leaning forward and taking notes and saying things like, "Yes!" and "That's right! Empowerment!" This was annoying.

"God will empower you toward your very own empire, ladies," the woman at the podium said with even more conviction. She motioned through the strategically opened blinds to her shiny pink Cadillac. "If you work hard, if you give it your all, if you believe, you could have a car just like it." The clappers began again. Elisa and I slipped out of there and found a back door. We smoked feverishly and then doused ourselves in Mary Kay's fresh, new spring scent.

Refining My Technique

During my stay at the Wells' home, I became adept at rationalizing my decision to run away. I was fifteen, and self-assured due to a deficiency of the fear that I now feel, merely reflecting. The Wells lived a few miles north of my childhood home, on a hilly, harmonious street; it was one of those suburban streets in Columbus, Ohio that I longed for and hated in equal measure. The street I now lived on had a name that ended with "wood" and unlike the Short North, there were rarely people walking down its middle but rather on the sidewalks, politely out of traffic's way. Interaction amongst neighbors consisted of little more than a nod and a wave. There was no yelling, no rhythmic bass escaping from parked cars, no soliciting—the street was quiet, uncomfortably so.

Rebellion feeds obdurate thoughts, giving them more purpose. My personal revolt was born during an argument with my father but it would soon prove pliability. I would soon turn against the Wells' matriarch, Miss Sarah, a person I was initially so grateful to for taking me in.

I worked for Miss Sarah to "earn my keep" by handing out business cards and collecting phone numbers in day-long mall recruitments. She told me not to waste my time with the "real pretty" and "real ugly" girls I saw. "The best clients are the ones with that one major flaw. That way, they see actual improvement and buy more of the product. Pick the girls with the bad skin, the big nose, the small eyes, the fat face...." She went on. She showed me how to apply blush at an angle in order to add dimension to a round face; conversely, if the face was too narrow, there was a lightening product that was applied to soften contours and draw attention away from severe chin lines or high foreheads. I would utilize these skills later, but at the time the knowledge just made me more self-conscious about myself. I no longer left the house—any house—without makeup. Cliché or no, I can honestly say that I felt naked without it, reliant on the foundation's mask-like quality that gave me perfectly clear skin, the lip liner that gave my lips more pout. Nonetheless, I had no desire to share my addiction to makeup with other girls.

It was not only disturbing to make such pilgrimages to the mall, but to do so was to pretend that my own insecurities did not exist. I would recite the very script Miss Sarah gave me, stating it bullet point for bullet point: "This is the best product available. There is a patent pending formula designed for that perfect, smooth skin you've always wanted." And I would apply makeup to girl's faces with a shaky hand, hoping they would actually look better by the time I was finished. Meanwhile, the girl I was speaking to would either look down shyly, extend her hand for a business card—that I imagined she would take home, stain with tears of inadequacy, and then ball up in a fit of never-mind-rage—or she would stare at my own troubled skin and say no. Some just walked away as soon as I began the pitch. I was better at bussing tables, and I began to regret the fact that I had gone AWOL from that job when I left the south side of town. My decision to leave had been mere logistics. The encounter between Mr. Emer and me had been something that caused me to leave abruptly enough that I had neglected to grab my name badge and smock. I had also forgotten my notebook, which had my scatter-shot weekly schedule. I took this as a sign that I was not supposed to be at that job any longer. It must have been divine intervention of some sort, I'd originally thought. Now, I felt a pang of regret.

***

"I'll throw you a few sales," Elisa offered. "Mom is frustrated with you, you know that, right?"

"Don't worry about it," I said.

"Sure?" She pointed to my bag. "You haven't collected any numbers all week. Have you sold anything at all?"

"A lipstick."

"Just one lipstick?"

"I know. Look, maybe I'm just not a great salesperson." I pushed out my bottom lip in a sarcastic pout. She understood my sarcasm, and appreciated it. Her appreciation for my sarcasm had become the backbone of our friendship—we shared a similar feeling of disdain for most things, as well as the shared belief that we were incredibly insightful.

I suppose the best way to describe my general mood then would be to say that I was less interested in most things than most people. It was simple, really, and common—a mild case of depression and anxiety—but then it seemed so perplexing and lonely. Elisa understood my disdain. She had jokes to compensate.

"You should sell some moisturizer to your ugly-ass boyfriend," she said, punching me lightly in the arm. She laughed at her own cleverness.

"I tried," I said. "He doesn't have any money."

James and I still talked on the phone, late at night, but we rarely saw each other anymore. Technically, we were still dating, but I didn't much care one way or the other. I had confided in Elisa that his father had groped me, but she had spun this in a way to make it James's fault. "He shouldn't have let you stay at home alone with his father, when he knows that old man is a sexual deviant." There had been a few times that Elisa met me at James's home while I stayed there and her conversations with James ping ponged between comic banter—jokes about his being underweight, her being over—and outright verbal stabbing that would end in Elisa storming off to the bus stop crying and me running after her only to return to James asking me endless questions about why I always defended that bitch, threatening to beat her like a man if she ever showed up in his home again.

The thing they had in common, a mutual love of quality marijuana, would usually erase these fights with their next encounter. Then, the weed smoke would fade, the cycle would repeat. Actually, Elisa's disdain of him was so severe that I felt it had rubbed off on me.

The truth was that I had been somewhat cold toward him since leaving. I never told him exactly what happened because I didn't care to, and I knew it would cause an explosive fight with Mr. Emer. The bottom line was that James didn't interest me as much. He was part of my past now, a past I would've preferred to leave behind, but he kept showing up, everywhere I went. I remember Elisa begging me to leave him. Maybe she had a sense of what was going to happen next, the compromise that would inevitably come between us and alienate me from her family. Or maybe she just didn't like him.

"I think I need to drop him," I agreed.

"Praise Jesus." She clapped her hands together and jumped up, which caused an older couple who were passing by us to walk around with an extra wide side step. She shuffled her feet in a sort of victory dance, then sat back down, out of breath, and lifted an inhaler to her lips.

"Yep, I'm finally sick of him. And, to be honest, I'm sick of selling this shit, too," I held up the bag, dangling it for her taking. She looked at it and then threw her own on the ground.

"I'm sick of this shit, too," she said. We sat there for a moment, watching people walk by, around our strewn makeup as though they didn't see it. Then she turned to me, smiled—her perfect, white teeth framed by round cheeks that were painted with diagonal slices of blush, blended to give the appearance of natural shading, defined cheekbones. She popped the cap off a fresh prescription of antidepressants and took two, swallowing them dry. She raised the bottle in the air as though it were a toast, and said, "Fuck James!"

We spent the next few hours roaming the mall and bad-mouthing not only James, but the entire south side of town, until, strangely enough—strange to us then, but looking back, he was always at the mall)—he appeared. He was walking with a large, lazy-eyed kid named Robert whom I had met once and found to be polite and charming. He would always tell me bar jokes (a hamburger walked into a bar...) and refill my glass as I sat in a circle, passing a blunt, taking shit from the rest of James's friends about how I wouldn't partake (…and the bartender says, "hey, we don't serve food."). I would laugh heartily, gasping for air at such jokes—probably thanks to a perpetual contact buzz—and ask him to tell me another, which he would.

That day in the mall, Robert took one look at Elisa and I swear I could see his knees buckle. Elisa rolled her long-lashed eyes at him in disgust, but she shook his hand when he extended it and shook it vigorously. He laughed and told her she had the strongest handshake he'd ever felt, female or no.

James hugged me and handed me a lighter. "You girls want to smoke?"

"No." I stood there, arms akimbo, wanting to know why he always asked me when he knew I'd say no.

"No?" Robert looked at Elisa in feigned disbelief.

James smiled, "Come on, Elisa, you like to smoke. It's been a while."

"No," I said.

"You want to drink? Robert lives pretty close, we could walk."

"Okay," Elisa said, taking me by surprise.

"Are you kidding?" I pulled her aside. "You can't drink with those pills. Besides, you don't even like James. You know if I go it'll be like I'm going back on everything we were just saying."

"I know, but I want a drink. We've been out here all day. Let's just go. It's better than selling Mary Kay."

"You got me there," I said. Suddenly, I was unable to think of much outside of how sweet a cold wine cooler would taste. We didn't want to drag our big Mary Kay bags around with us on the walk, so we went into the last stall of the women's restroom and stuck the bags behind the toilet. The City Center Mall was never very busy; and even if it was, we figured, how many people look behind a toilet during the day?

On the walk, which turned out to be almost thirty minutes long, Robert did most of the talking. James was rapping along with some song that blasted through his Walkman and I was doing my best to ignore him.

During our trek, I asked Robert about his limp. I wasn't used to seeing him out of context, walking. He was always sitting at home when I saw him. "Does your foot hurt or something?"

He said that his father had backed over him in a truck and busted up his hip. I became enthralled as he told his story. I watched him tell it as we walked, appreciating how he watched Elisa for her response to his each word.

"I was working with Dad on a twelve-hour trip," he began. "I had been driving most the way and when I let him take the wheel I was so tired I didn't even know we were out of gas. He asked me to pump. I went to the bathroom, but it was getting cold so I decided to get my coat out of the back of the truck. I opened the door and reached inside. Before I knew it the truck's weight was pushing me, and after feeling like I could hold the weight for a second, I fell over and woke up in the ER."

His father had said he thought Robert had walked away from the truck to get cigarettes and that's why he backed up. He said he was going to drive up closer to the gas station, go in himself, get coffee; that he didn't even think to check if Robert was still pumping; he was tired, too. It wasn't the truck itself that Robert had felt weighing on him, but three of the stolen pallets they were transporting. They'd fallen on him when the truck backed up with open doors. Robert's dad collected disability for his own ailment (no one knew what) and supplemented his income by driving more "found" moving pallets to an unknown destination in Cleveland.

I wonder how Robert is doing now. He was one of those people that seemed to get one bad break after another, and I wondered why when he seemed so genuinely kind and intelligent. I think there's a good chance Robert might've decided to quit working for his father one day, go to school, do something. Then again, he very well may be in that same living room, smoking, drinking, coughing, fading.

When someone got really drunk he was "faded." At Robert's house we drank half a bottle of vodka and mixed it with orange juice; it was hardly enough to get me faded. A bag of White Castle sliders and chicken rings on the table, James and I were left in a front room. We were kissing, something I couldn't do with him anymore unless I was drunk. I remember feeling nauseated and wondering if it was due to the smell of the onion burgers, or James's proximity. Why did I kiss him if I wasn't into it?

Elisa and Robert emerged from the bedroom hand-in-hand, new lovers, though they had only kissed, she said. We didn't have enough for a cab home and too much time had passed to go back to the mall and retrieve our makeup, so we weighed our options and ended up deciding that the best thing would be to get more alcohol. We drank until we were tired; the last time I looked at the clock it said six a.m. When we did go back, I received my eviction notice. Miss Sarah told me I could sleep on the couch that night, but to get my "bony ass" out of her house the next morning or she'd call the police. And don't talk to her daughter again. I agreed.

As I said my goodbyes the next morning, Elisa waited for Miss Sarah to look away before mouthing, "I'll find you."

I mouthed back, "Teen center."

I walked toward the bus stop and as soon as the COTA pulled up I felt somehow free again. I hadn't slept. It was almost Christmas time and I had no other choice.

Looking back, it is as though my childhood were a movie screen, me the all-knowing viewer, screaming, "Go home," at the protagonist, the dumb, prideful teenager.

Then, there was no question. Calling home, apologizing to my Dad for our fight, asking for help—none of it occurred to me. I knew what to do then. I called James. I no longer considered myself a runaway—this was my life. Or so I told myself then.

James, in usual fashion, met me at the bus stop. I wouldn't go back to his house, not even when he told me his father wouldn't be there. I said it wasn't his father but some other reason that I couldn't explain. He knew a few people who hung out at the teen center, so he said he'd join me there.

When we arrived, hands clasped tight, a couple of the counselors walked up to me and introduced themselves to James. The usual group of kids was hanging out in the back of the room, some playing pool and some sitting on the couches, talking. They all stared at us. Damien was among them. The last time I saw Damien was shortly before I ran away. He had stolen my Walkman and pushed me down after school, daring me to punch him so he could hit me back. He was one reason I didn't want to go back to school, a contributing factor in my reasoning behind leaving Dad's house, the neighborhood, which might make my runaway tale a bit more reasonable—nah. I prefer the more romantic: genetic predisposition, misplaced anger, depression, under-developed frontal lobe.

"I won't hit a girl first," Damien kept saying that day, as he punched me in the arm on my way home from school, leaving bruises. His friends, boys I didn't know laughed, thinking he wasn't hitting me hard. I was good at holding in tears; I was tough.

One time Damien flashed me his penis, another time he flashed me a gun. He liked to show me things, to see me cower in the same way he liked to see his mark on whoever he dated.

"That's him," I said to James, happy to allow him to take action now, "the boy who stole my Walkman."

"I know Damien," James said and walked straight up to him. Damien towered six inches or more above James, and for a moment I lost faith in the myth that James could fight. I wanted to look away, but then, a solid jab knocked Damien to the ground. Two more hits landed near his head, which he cradled in his arms. And, almost just as quickly as I was able to process these events, the two counselors that had just introduced themselves were hauling James out the door.

"I didn't know he was going to do that," I promised them. They pulled me by my arm. "Can I come back? I don't really have anywhere else to go," I said. I had been planning to ask someone there if they knew of a place for me to stay. Now I was ousted, an enemy of the teen center I used to frequent every day after school, before I dropped out.

As I stood dumbstruck in front of the building, James yelled at me to follow him. I didn't want to, but there was something demanding in his voice, something I wasn't used to. I wanted to apologize to everyone; I was to blame here, after all. I ran back inside the center and said that I was sorry. I even apologized to Damien who responded by running toward me and pushing me to the ground. He put me in some sort of headlock and spun me around as I wondered why everyone was so quick to get James off him, but seemed to be taking their time rescuing me. "Stop!" It was all I could think to say.

"Dumb bitch," he said. He let me go, and I felt anger well up inside me. I looked into his brown eyes, dilated pupils, and I ran toward him. I swung and swung, landing on piles of air, until, finally, impact. I found impact again, and realized that I couldn't stop. Damien pushed me off and sent me skidding on my butt backwards, toward the wall.

"Wow," I heard James yell out from the door. "That's my girl." The counselors yelled at him again.

"I'm not leaving so you all can let my girl get beat up!" There. Maybe James wasn't so bad.

As I was escorted out, this time probably for good, I heard someone say I was tough.

Everything gets blurry after a fight, blurry and clear at the same time—the high of adrenaline, which no drug I've tried has been able to match. The competing forces of adrenaline and fatigue, even after such a short fight, made me confident that I had nothing to worry about. I had been worried about where I would go next, and suddenly it didn't matter. James and I would celebrate.

James. He was all I had. We found Elisa and Robert at the White Castle by her house. They said they had been planning to meet us at the center after a bite to eat.

Robert asked me to sit next to him. I did, and he threw a heavy arm around me with his other arm around Elisa. "So, girls, let's see if you know this one. How do you turn a dishwasher into a snowplow?" he said this as he pointed to the window. It was snowing lightly outside. We didn't know. "Give that bitch a shovel."

"You ass," Elisa said.

I pushed Robert away and moved back to the opposite side of the booth. I watched Elisa and Robert devour their onion burgers and kiss; James and I laughed at how disgusting it was to kiss after one of those burgers. "They're in love," James whispered. We exchanged a look of joyous disbelief. Even on fucked up days like this, I thought, some strange kind of beauty is possible.

"So what's up, ya'll?" Robert asked, turning from his beloved. "You two will not believe what just happened." James and I exchanged a look of brief but mutual understanding as we listened.

Elisa had left home. She announced, proudly, that she was now a fellow runaway. James laughed and made some comment about how he and Robert would probably run away, too, if they had anything to run from, or to.

Apparently, Miss Sarah forbade Elisa to go out because she was afraid her daughter was going out with me, or, worse, on a date with Robert. She had met Robert because Elisa invited him over for lunch, introducing him as a friend, but Miss Sarah knew better. She could see the adoration in his eyes and had refused to let him in the house, calling him a knucklehead, no better than me. Miss Sarah was mortified by her daughter's choice to date Robert, Elisa explained. My friend decided she'd had enough of her mother telling her who she could hang out with and who she couldn't. She said that her mother screamed at her from the porch, and ultimately, Elisa just left, stating that it was for good. Maybe I *had* influenced her.

Even back then, I had been able to glamorize my story. In fact, I was living in a constant state of mental wreckage. I was sick, and growing sicker in the alcohol-induced coma I was beginning to maintain. I was a transient teen with no money, little confidence, and a constant level of dread and despondence that was only subdued by the adrenaline of moving on. And, worse yet, I wasn't even running away from anything horrible. Dad didn't hit me. Mom didn't sign me up for beauty pageants. I had left home to leave myself, and it hadn't worked. Now it was too late to go back. Now, it was almost Christmas.

Elisa was excited, telling me how she had rebelled, stood up for herself, finally.

"That sounds familiar," I told her.

"You should have seen her face! I even said I wanted to marry Robert and then we walked off laughing, just to piss her off, you know. And you know what she said?" Elisa stood up and imitated Miss Sarah, arms akimbo. "'How could you pick someone so ugly? He's dark as fucking night Elisa! He's lazy-eyed! You want a baby that looks like that? With your pretty hair? With your face? Are you insane?' Can you believe I put up with her shit? Sold her makeup for her every weekend? Can you believe she actually said that, right in front of him?"

"Yes."

That night we all got drunk and ended up at another one of James's friend's house. We were attempting to celebrate. We thought we were freeing ourselves from the roles we knew: daughter, martyr. We were taking control of our lives and holding our ground. Now we just needed to find the next place to live.

***

I woke up cold, on a porch on the north side of town with paper plates all around me. Bottles and ashtrays were everywhere. I missed the warmth of Elisa's home, of my home. I had been listening to someone's Walkman when I fell asleep. I was shivering, with a dull ache in my ear from the place where I had slept heavily against the plastic earpiece. I walked into the house for some water; James was on another couch inside the house, sleeping. I crept past him, past Elisa, past Robert, asleep on the floor. There was a swell in my throat as I drank, directly from the tap. The after-party scene of the house, my friends passed out drunk, the rotten smell of stale food and malt liquor all revolted me now. I looked around for my backpack.

I didn't think about leaving Elisa or James, I couldn't think of anything but leaving. Well, that and warmth. I walked through the angry winter air, dazed, and to a payphone where I dialed my father's phone number, collect. I don't know what possessed me, but I was overcome, unable to stop myself and reconsider the actions I was taking. When my father picked up I hesitated.

"Dad?" There was a silence, but one that made my body feel heavy. It was a silence allowed to me, a generous gift. "Can you come and get me?"

My father said yes and the heaviness lifted, immediately replaced by a nervous anticipation that I tried to walk off; I paced back and forth. I was on the corner of Cleveland Avenue and McKinley, only blocks away from the high school I would have been thinking of had I never run away. I would have been reaching, exasperatingly, for the snooze button on my alarm clock and having to actually get out of bed to reach it. Then, when my feet would hit the floor, I wouldn't be able to return to sleep and I would begin to search for the right thing to wear, anticipating my day: the sleepy bus ride, the boring, long periods of Homeroom and Spanish, the lunch hour of smoking behind the track or taking off early to find a COTA to the teen center.

I paced, somehow sure that I would never return to the reality I used to have. Returning home didn't mean going back to how things were, I thought. As I tried to imagine what it would be like, I heard a horn sound. A sharp Cadillac slowed down and turned at the corner across the street. This was not a good corner to stand on at this time of day, and when the Cadillac circled back a second time, honking again, I surmised the driver's intentions were that I go around the corner and meet him for an interlude. *I'm underage, you fuck.* These thoughts, of how I was being seen—or how I thought I was been seen—exasperated the budding knowledge that I had good reason to feel shame. The world was angry at me for being a fuckup, and this fact was reiterated by the rushed sound of each passing car, the pang of imagined thoughts as drivers passed by. The occasional birdsong that came from a nearby park reminded me how far I'd run, how toxic I'd become. I considered walking back to James then, but I was too tired to move.

My father arrived in a junky Honda CRX that made its presence known with the hesitant growl and hum of its settling engine. I walked to the car and stood briefly at the driver's side window. My father watched me from behind the glass, as though I were feral now, and he would have to move slowly, cautiously measuring my reaction. He rolled down the window, and told me to get in. The invitation was a relief.

Once inside the car, we sat there, parked for a moment. My father could see that I was dirty, probably reeking of beer and smoke. I watched him, emotions dancing across his face; an ephemeral expression of pure joy settling into relief, and then serious contemplation. Neither of us spoke. I knew that it was up to me, but when I tried to speak, something stopped me. Instead, I clasped my hands in my lap and watched them intently as my father began to drive. *I'm sorry*, I thought, I said.

What *would* he do with me, he asked. *The hell if I know.*

First Diagnosis

It was 1995 when I returned home to my father. Mom had her own apartment, which Laura and I would walk to on Wednesdays. We carried backpacks full of clothes and toiletries because she didn't have a washing machine or room to accommodate too many of our clothes. On Saturdays, we would walk back. We kept most of our stuff at Dad's—his house, after all, had all the amenities that Mom's one-bedroom loft lacked.

I returned to school, but I didn't stay. Just wandering around the halls, resting my feet in classrooms, watching other kids act out, a teacher's blood pressure visibly rise, a jaw piercing bell sound—I think I made it to third period that first day back before ducking out the door by the track and walking to the nearest bus stop. Something wasn't right with me, I told my parents, separately. That's why I ran away. I wanted them to know that I was sick. Sick was my self-diagnosis. Television had assisted with my hypothesis, egging me on by the increased number of legal mind-altering drugs. No one should suffer, commercials announced between re-runs of *Saved by the Bell*. I listened.

Psychopharmacology had become all the rage, or at least I noticed it then. Pills promised to tinker with brain chemistry of wayward teens and offer a modern-day cure to age-old ailments. It was at this time that my father was beginning to make better money at work. I had returned home because I wanted to start anew, reestablish myself as the good daughter. The first time I considered medicine, I considered it from an experimental point of view. I was almost seventeen and my reestablishing had its limits. I remember hoping that antidepressant pills would be as fun as getting drunk was.

Elisa was on a few prescriptions, and I had asked her about them often. When she first started them, she had explained that the pills made her feel disconnected. She had said it felt as though she hovered above herself, watching, unable to self-edit. They also caused her to get drunk faster, thereby saving her money. I said I wanted that. The way I saw it, my editing process was on overdrive, and who couldn't use a cheaper means of drunkenness?

Dad offered—possibly, he insisted; the exact nature of this suggestion, I don't remember—to take me to a rehabilitation program for neighborhood teens with "problems," and I remember thinking, *Why the hell not?* It was what I wanted; it was the trendy thing to do. He made sure to show me the price of entry, explaining how much of his salary that was. He was barely able to scrape together the cost, he'd said, but anything for his little girl. Before agreeing, I considered my options.

Things between me and both parents had been awkward since my return. A perpetual guilt trailed me, no matter how much I apologized. What clenched my willingness to embark on this adventure was my mother, who, when I had asked if she thought it was a good idea said, "It'd really mean a lot to me, honey. And to your father. He isn't there, is he?"

"I'm doing this, then. I probably won't see you for a while, Mom. Check in would be tomorrow and we're not allowed guests."

My body stiffened as I walked to the desk where I would check in at Ohio State University's mental health center that first day. Dad reminded me that he couldn't get his money back. This would be good for me; it was what I wanted. I walked in, feeling as I had years before, when Dad insisted I start running; I had brought this on. I had no say.

**

I had tried to fight only once before with my father. I stood in the parking lot with my arms crossed defensively, rigid, pitifully trying to stand my ground as Dad instructed me to run. We were at Schiller, a twenty-three acre park just south of downtown, and my father's idea was to complete one loop around, about a mile. The smell of pastries wafted around the thick, summer air as I stood. I remember feeling dumbstruck and swindled. I had only agreed to go to the park, not to run a mile. I widened my stance.

My father laughed and said, "You're going to run today, eventually."

Left with this, I knew my only other way out was to evoke pity; after all, I *was* his little girl. I began to cry, beg. I heaved between sobs, asking why I had to do this and my sister didn't. I was eight years old, a somewhat plump child with no desire to run, and I explained this. My father, in turn, lifted his ankle and began to twist, confounding me with his ability to ignore my loud display of protest. "You're running a mile today."

A woman walking in the park stopped to glance at me; I was sitting on the ground, hugging my knees, red-faced, yelling, "No. I'm not going to run." She asked if everything was all right and my father smiled warmly and said that it was, the kid was just throwing a fit. She looked hesitant, but walked on. My father stood at his full six feet, hovering above me, waiting with tireless patience until my butt and legs were too numb to sit any longer. I adjusted, but continued to cry, continued to hold my chest tightly. I screamed again, hoping someone more assertive would come to my rescue, but passers-by could see him keeping his distance, stretching as if nothing were wrong. They believed his body language, not mine. He waited until my tears were all drained. He waited until the sky began to darken, which, when looking back on it now seemed like forever—but seeing as how we had gone out after he got off of work at five, it had probably been no longer than an hour. I stood and stretched, careful not to make eye contact or acknowledge the man who was being so cruel. I had finally decided to run, if only to get back home and cry again, safely, in my mother's arms. My mother would understand his stubbornness, the way it could injure a person.

"You're going to do this, and then you'll be done," he said. "Come on." He grabbed my arm and jerked it forward as he began to jog, slowly.

Ultimately, with red, raw eyes, I would run, walk, jog, and then run again to get the thing over with. As we began, moving past a picnic area and a pond, I summoned more tears, but it was harder to breathe when I cried, so I tried to man up. We jogged by the pond where I wanted to stop, to search the water for fish, but my dad said, "Later." I jogged quicker, alongside him now, not conscious of where I was going. I had never been so deep into the park. The trees were thicker for a long stretch which led, gloriously, to a gazebo. I asked if I could walk to the gazebo and my father conceded. We walked quickly, probably quicker than we had been jogging, and as soon as we hit our mark, my father clapped. "Let's go." We began to run, faster than before.

As my feet began to quicken, one after another, covering more of the flat path that led to sidewalk, my father began to cheerlead. "You're doing great, Jen. You're a natural runner. And after this, we can go out for ice cream."

"I just want to go home," I wheezed.

"You really have natural form," he went on. "Look at me," he wriggled around and let his arms fall to his sides as though they had no life; they looked like wet towels, flopping against his sides as he took awkward, exaggerated steps. I tried to stifle a laugh. "And look at you. You look like Flo-Jo." This was a calculated move that I didn't pick up on at the time. I had always loved watching the Olympics with my father, and I especially liked to watch Florence Griffith Joyner, her wildly-painted nails and fantastic grace. As much as I still hated my father for forcing me to run, I felt my pace pick up, a shot of momentum came with the comparison that told me to ignore my slight difficulty breathing; even the uncomfortable movement of running after a tiring day at school seemed easier when I imagined my own body could imitate greatness such as hers. He was tricking me, but all I could think was *what if he was right?*

For the first time in my life, at eight years old, I realized what it was to be high on pure endorphins. I was overwhelmed by the rush in my blood, which seemed to cleanse my thoughts and exacerbate the sweetness of accomplishment when we rounded that last turn and headed back toward the car. My father's praise hadn't stopped since we began to run, and I accepted it as an energizing soundtrack to the meditative ride home. He had smiled at me at every stop light. "You did good, kiddo," he said. "That mile took us thirteen minutes. But one day, you'll be able to do it in ten, then eight, maybe even six."

"Do you think I could really be good?" I asked, forgetting everything that preceded our run, forgetting the tears, the waiting, the sharp pull on my arm.

"I really do."

From that day forward, my father and I ran three days a week, after he got home from work. A few years later, I won first place in the girl's twelve and under category of the *Circleville Classic,* a five mile race (that I'm still proud to have completed in less than 40 minutes!) Dad was satisfied by my unquenchable pride, my jumping, energetic bliss. He had given me something to be confident about.

I remember tracing the gold-plated female figure of the runner that was balanced at the top of a wood-colored platform, lined with gold, my prize. I held it close to my chest, savoring the day: I had been photographed with the announcer, cheered for being so young, for getting such a good time—under eight minutes each mile.

***

Sixteen years old, now fashionably rebellious and always ready to run, I looked around at the sand colored walls and pale green gowns that lethargic teenagers wore as they walked past me. I thought about what my own decision-making had got me, and I decided I better have a go at this thing. Meanwhile, though, I couldn't get around the oddness of these kids: they all seemed to have extreme, cartoon-like shapes, many of the girls were dangerously underweight, their limp arms seemed to have less range; others were obese and sloppy. The mucky mixture of stale, hospital air and body odor lingered in my nose. Some of these kids glanced at me, but most seemed to have no interest whatever. Dark circles encased a set of eyes that I locked. These eyes belonged to a boy with a mess of long, tangled hair that extended to his shoulders. When I smiled at him, the eyes averted. I laughed. Was I supposed to sleep here?

I was sure now that this was not the help I wanted. If there was help at a place like this hospital it was for people with *real* problems. These kids were drugged up sociopaths, and I didn't belong. Maybe I would do better fixing myself or even listening to my father for just another year; I'd done it for this long. Maybe I could take up running again; the endorphins might help me now. I would even quit smoking.

Dad must have seen my hesitation. He hugged me, stating again that the pressing inconvenience of this expense was well worth it for his little girl. His scent, the earthy olive oil soap he used, was comforting compared to the smells of the hospital. I turned. "This is wrong, I can feel it," I said. But the deposit was done, and the papers were signed.

"You did the crime," he said. I would have to do my time. I was equally guilt-ridden and grateful. I apologized to my father, and as he walked away, I thanked him.

The program introduced me to a vocabulary similar to that used in penitentiaries. We (the patients) were allowed phone privileges after we completed our daily exercises (art, stretching, mantras, and group talk) that were supposed to help "rehabilitate" us. I called Elisa the second day to apologize for leaving her with Robert and James. As I suspected, she was already back at home, safe and sound. No hard feelings, she promised.

"Elisa, they have us doing ceramics. I made a goddamn ceramic dog today! The eyes are kind of weird…," I said this as I turned the freshly baked dog in my hands, wondering if such activities actually helped anyone, and, if so, how?

"We need to get you out of there," Elisa said. "Ceramic-dog-making is considered torture in some cultures."

"I think so," I said. The phone clicked twice, meaning I only had one minute left to talk. "There's my signal. Hey, how are you and Robert doing?"

"I'm thinking about breaking up with him."

"What? I thought you all were in love. Why?"

"Mom said that if I don't, she'll cut off my trust fund,"

"Why does she hate him so much?"

"Why do you think? He's too dark, too black—" The phone cut her off, and I was left to wonder why Miss Sarah could dislike anyone for a characteristic so similar to her own. Elisa got her light skin from her father, a quiet Puerto Rican man who rarely moved from his Lazy Boy chair and spoke less than ten words to me when I lived there, two of them being "get out."

***

A few days into my time, the boy with the shoulder length hair offered to show me the cuts that extended up his arms. I supposed I deserved this unwanted attention since I had made the mistake of smiling at him. We sat across from each other in a common area where there were coffee tables filled with books that were supposedly filled with uplifting stories, stories of redemption and promise. One of the counselors suggested I read any time I had free. "I'll look at your arm," I said, vaguely curious. *Why the fuck would a person cut himself on the arm when he could just go for the wrist and avoid all this*? I thought mockingly.

"What will you give me if I show them to you?" I decided this kid was an idiot.

"Fuck you, I don't really care. I was humoring you." He lifted his sleeve to expose some unremarkable red lines that extended from the inside of his elbow to his lower forearm. "Why did you do that?"

"It's fun. It's like a release. It makes you feel like you're clean again, like you've flushed out all the toxins in your body," he said, now smiling.

"Bullshit. Why not just give blood? The Red Cross always needs donors."

The boy told me to fuck myself before walking away, and a counselor wearing a pale blue polo shirt and creased khakis approached me. "What did you say to him?" he asked.

"I told him cutting was ridiculous. It's the dumbest shit I've ever heard of."

"And why do you think you are in a place to judge him?" he asked, taking the seat the boy had just left. It was a good question and I told him so. I told him I didn't feel like I belonged; he explained that everyone felt that way. The important thing was not comparison but self-reflection. This was my time to work on me.

Reality bit me hard as I sat there, allowing him to speak, sure of how wrong he was. I felt that my dismissal of this kid's plea for attention might just be the thing to cure him. I thought maybe my tough love would cure many of these kids if I stayed here long enough. They were just desperate for attention; they didn't share my logic or reasoning. I had good reason to leave home. On the drive to the facility, my father said that he wasn't surprised I'd run away. He said that I needed to come out of my shell and if I would have done so earlier, my desire to prove myself independent wouldn't have built up so much and I wouldn't have had to go through such lengths.

Mine was a reason of pure logic. I wanted freedom. These kids wanted people to take care of them and what they really needed was a person like my father, to hover and show them the other side of things. When the man finally left me to my internal dialogue, I decided not to speak to anyone else during my stay, but after a couple of days, I began to engage the cutter in conversation regularly. His name was Brian, and as his dark hair grew during time served, I could see that his hair was naturally blonde, better suiting his freckled complexion. He said he had rich parents who took a lot of vacations and that he hated them for being rich. "Money just corrupts people," he said.

"Poverty corrupts people, too," I said. He didn't argue. Instead, he asked me what books I'd recently read. It was an unexpected question, one that made my face warm with a rush of embarrassment

"I don't really read that much anymore. I've been too distracted," I said. Brian gave me a list of books to read: *The Catcher in the Rye*, *On the Road*, *Fear and Loathing in Las Vegas*, and *The Bell Jar*. "Books speak to me," he said. "It's just good to know that other people suffer, too. In my life outside of here, with my parents, even my friends, it seems like no one believes that I can't just change, just like that." He snapped his fingers.

The fact that I could relate to this kid bothered me. I had come to realize that the counselors believed I was just another runaway, a troubled teen wanting attention. After all, there I was, wearing a pale green hospital dress over jeans and a tank top, depleting my father's bank account in exchange for what? I had spent nights on a cardboard-like cot, unable to close my door more than halfway, so that nurses could check on me every few hours. I had eaten bread pudding with a spork, and made a ceramic dog. I decided then that I was ready to go. I would go through the motions, say what the counselors wanted to hear, whatever would get me through. Brian said he wished he'd have tried this strategy as well. He was being released the next day and all he could think about was getting fucked up with his friends. I thanked him for the list that day, and we exchanged numbers that we'd never dial.

I hovered at around the phone, waiting for one of my fellow crazies to get off the phone. It was two days before my release, and I had done as planned, gone through the activities numbly, answered questions predictably, and, as a result, I was allowed extra phone privileges. I looked around to make sure no one was waiting and then dialed my mother's new phone number.

My sister answered on the first ring.

"Hey, Laura."

"Jailbird!" She laughed her "heh-eh-eh" of a laugh. "How are you? Is the crazy wearing off yet?"

She was being kind, I thought, *I should recognize that.* "Shut up, Laura. Put Mom on the phone."

"Fine. Don't drop the crazy soap, heh-eh…." She went on laughing until I told her to shut up, then she dropped the phone on something hard, *clunk*.

"Hello," Mom's soft voice offered itself to me.

"Mom. Hi," I felt guilt punching at me repeatedly as I spoke. "I, uh...I heard you were sick. How are you feeling?" My father called to tell me my mother had a panic attack earlier that day. He said it wasn't serious but that I should be extra nice to her.

"The doctors said it was stress-induced, and you know how things always hit me after the fact. He also said my blood pressure is too high," she explained. I knew it was my fault. How could she be anything but stressed? She had a "runaway" daughter who had been admitted to a teen intervention center. "I'm feeling much better," she said. She sounded shaky; she sounded sweet. "How are *you*, honey?" she asked.

"Do you have a library card, Mom?" She said that she did, and inquired about the sorts of life skills I was learning in the program.

"Well, I made a ceramic dog." She chuckled. "It's supposed to be some sort of therapy to do ceramics. Art 'brings you into the moment,' they say and 'allows you to release your pent up emotions.'" I mocked the nasally tone of the woman who had led this exercise. "Then we got in a circle and bitched about life and how horrible it is to be young and full of desire in a miserable world full of stifling restrictions and guilt-inducing unobtainable standards ...." I paused. "I don't feel as bad as the rest of these people, that's for sure. I think I'm ready to come home."

"Have you spoken to your father?"

"No."

"You should do that," *Click.* "He's the one paying for this, you know."

"Believe me, I know. And Mom, I want you to take care of yourself. I love you. And I'm really sorry if I'm stressing you out."

"It's not just you, baby. It's been everything, the divorce, everything."

"I know," I lied, "but I'll…" *Click.* "...stop."

I hung up the phone and returned to my pale room. I sat in my pale gown and rested my forehead in pale hands. I tried to cry but couldn't. I couldn't feel much of anything.

Ms. Randall, a wide, white nurse appeared in my doorway. "It is time for your session," she said. I followed her down a white hallway and into a small room with a huge desk sitting dead center. A man with glasses looked me over and told me to sit.

"This is your official exit interview, but before we release you, I want to ask a few questions. Okay, so, what is it that brought you here?"

"Nurse Betty."

He didn't flinch. "What exactly brought you to our facility?"

"I don't know. I don't like life too much, I guess."

"You sound rehearsed," he observed.

"I don't think I need to be here any longer. I realize that I made a mistake, running away. It's the first impulsive thing I've done like that. I mean, I learned my lesson."

"Well, according to the tests we've given you, you show no obvious signs of mental illness. I think you may just be depressed, maybe a little anxious. Or you're acting out?" He waited for me to respond, maybe agree, as I stared at the creases in his forehead. "If so, it'll pass. It's just angst."

I considered his words as though they were on a menu. I wanted him to give me pills like Elisa's. They made her confident in a manic sort of way. He said I didn't need them, and signed my release papers.

***

I handed the porcelain dog to my father in lieu of a hello when he picked me up. "This is what they had you do in there, huh? For all that money...."

"Yup. Check it out!" I held the eyeless brown dog in the air with mock pride. "And you thought you were the artist of the family."

He gave me a hug. This acceptance, I thought, would be all the medication I needed. And, as soon as the sappiness of this thought hit me, I hit it back, bringing my teenage brain back to its normal place in self-loathing and self-pity. I went to the corner store, where I was never asked of identification, and bought a few bottles of flavored beer so that I could stay up through the night and plan out my future.

This time at my father's home was filled with strange rules and even stranger allowances. For instance, I was now supposed to always eat dinner with the family, no matter what, but I could stay out pretty much as late as I wanted. I was never to leave my clothes scattered around my room, and the house should be vacuumed daily now, no exceptions. "We should keep this place spotless. There's no reason not to," Dad said. Meanwhile, when I told him I couldn't stomach high school, he said that was up to me but I had to promise to get my GED. Then again, he'd said, that was up to me, too. It felt like my father was walking on eggshells now, and yet he was maintaining his authority with this new clean house regime. His allowance to me, that I determine how to spend my own free time, seemed wrong, somehow, but I expressed gratitude.

It would be a few months before I would leave home again, this time for good. It would be years before I would give the world of psychology another shot. Even Dad admitted that maybe I was just restless. Maybe I was ready to be on my own. I had the distinct feeling that he was ready for me to go.

69

I wanted to go to college, but would have to make my own way. I told Dad this and he said that was good because he was going back to college to finish his bachelor's degree, as soon as he found the money. I was on my own financially, which didn't come as much of a surprise. What did was the day I moved out, when my father stopped me at the bottom of the stairs and gave me a hug. "Jen, I love you, but you earned your independence when you ran away. What I'm trying to say is that I can no longer help you financially with college." The fact that he would have otherwise helped me with college was news to me, news that stuck with me.

"Whatever. I want to do things myself anyhow," I said.

PART TWO:

THE DANCER

1997

I had moved back into my father's house only to move out again a few months later, this time on more agreeable terms. Two years after I ran away from him, it was his turn to leave.

By 1997 I was broke. I was living with my mother part-time, and with friends the rest of the time. So when Dad announced that he was selling his house and using his money to go back to college I felt another tremor in our relationship, which was still rather rickety. He would move away with his new wife—a woman whom I had yet to *know*, really take the time to get to know at this time—but because we had theoretically reconciled, I wished him luck as the adult I was, and I told him I was proud.

My mother's apartment was a one-bedroom flat with a kitchenette that didn't exactly lend itself to family dinners. Mom labored for longer and steadier hours than I'd ever seen, and she no longer spent hours on the phone with her NA friends. In fact, she'd found a position at a drug and alcohol treatment center where she was paid minimum wage to council those with addictions in need of an available ear, a comforting word. She excelled at the position, but the opportunity for advancement was slim.

My sister was in and out as much as I was by this time. When we were both there, she didn't seem eager to engage me in conversation and often ignored my inquiries about where she'd been, whether she had a boyfriend, where she stayed. In this apartment, it was my sister who monopolized the phone, spending hours locked away in the bathroom, laughing and carrying on about who-knows-what with who-knows-who.

At night, Mom insisted that we take the bedroom while she slept on the couch. This left my sister and me to sleep head-to-foot in the queen size bed, which often proved troublesome, even dangerous. When I woke up with one of my sister's restless size tens plunging toward my eye, I hadn't the chance to move before impact. We laughed briefly over the black eye that began to surface the next morning, but after this time I would avoid the bed at all costs, opting instead to create a nest of comforters and pillows in the small space between the foot of the bed and the closet door. It was here on the floor that I would write in my notebook each night, developing furtive plans for improving this situation.

I sat up, listening to my sister snore, watching her monstrous feet fidget in her sleep, her legs wrenching around as though she were kicking at hacky sacks in her sleep. "Laura," I whispered. When she didn't respond, I reached through the wooden bed frame and gripped her leg, which caused her to jerk away violently.

She awoke with a snort. "What the fuck?"

"Laura, quiet. Look, I just wanted to tell you that I'm going to move out soon. If I don't see you, I want you to take care of Mom, okay? I don't want you to just stop here and eat up all her food with your little ragamuffin friends, okay? I'm serious."

"Shut up, Jenny. Fuck. I'm trying to sleep."

"Look, I really think we should start trying to help out more around here when we stop by, you know? Mom seems so tired. She needs our help."

"I know." Laura sat up; her half-opened eyes searched my face. Her hair was cut into a short spiky style that she dyed black with purple tips. The quarter-sized plug in her ear matched her hair. I noticed that it was straining the lobe. "Did you go up a size?" I pointed to the plug.

She said she had, the plug was an eight-gauge and her ear would look angry for a few days. Then, impatiently, she asked, "How the hell are you going to move out? You get a new boyfriend or something?"

"No. I'm going to earn the money. Somehow. Look, it doesn't matter. Point is, I made up my mind. I'm sick of watching Mom look so miserable all the time. She deserves better. Will you back me up? Just be there for her, okay? Don't use her up."

"I'm there for Mom," she said defensively. Her body fell backwards, landing on the mattress with a thump. "Are you going to let me sleep now?" she asked.

"Goodnight, Laura."

"Jenny, sorry about the black eye last week," she added with a soft chuckle. A beat later, in a quiet voice she added, "Oh, James called for you again last week."

"Next time he does, tell him I moved," I said. It had been months since I'd spoken to James, and he had become no more than a minor annoyance, a part of my past that I couldn't seem to shake.

That night, I stayed up, thinking. I decided that I needed to follow my father's example. I, too, craved a reformation. I thought money would be the way to accomplish this, and I began to amass a list of ways I could acquire the funds needed to move out, allow my mother the space she deserved; or at the very least, contribute to the rent.

It didn't take long before I had a quick-money plan. I was seventeen now, and I knew that the difference between being broke, which was temporary, and being poor, which was permanent, was either family money or education. I had no access to family money, so I set my sights on college. As soon as I turned eighteen, I would obtain my GED and sign up for courses at college. Dad had the right idea, it seemed. So how do I get to college? What about the meantime?

***

The advertisements said "Dancers/Models Wanted" as though stripping and modeling were interchangeable professions. There would almost always be somewhere between three and nine dollar symbols below the words, suggesting unlimited earning potential. My only worry was whether I would have the nerve.

I dialed the number below the dollar symbols. A girl named Angel told me to stop by anytime between noon and four the next day for an audition, and just ask for Barry. I thanked her and hung up the phone.

There I was for the rest of the day, fantasizing about what such a career path would lead to. What does a stripper look like? I asked the mirror. Taller, the mirror said, with longer hair. Blonde hair. So, I flat-ironed my hair until it resembled straw, slapped on my Payless heels, and spent the rest of the morning dancing in front of my half-length bathroom mirror. I had to stand on the toilet to watch my ass sway and then jump back down to watch my shoulders. I tried for a sexy, circular motion. This is what I would do on my audition. This is what I'd wear.

The next day, hours fled by as I yanked out my heels again and traced thick lines, the same light shade of blue, around my eyes. I practiced what I might say when introducing myself. "I'm new at this, but I learn fast." "I used to dance, but it's been a while, so no laughing." Then again, I had to be business-like, in case the place was too sleazy or I felt uncomfortable. If you don't give a fuck, no one will want to fuck with *you*, James used to tell me. I almost called him in an ephemeral moment of longing, but I couldn't imagine his reaction to my desire to strip, and I didn't want to.

It was almost three o'clock. I grabbed my backpack and put on a short gray skirt that I rarely wore. I walked to the corner store. A bottle of Boones Farm strawberry wine and a bottle of Snapple, and I would be ready to go. The thick man behind the counter said, "Where are you going, pretty lady?" And I told him to mind his own business, thinking I looked good, good. Irrationally, I felt as though he knew where I was going. I dumped the Snapple's contents out in the front of the store and refilled the bottle. The strawberry-flavored wine went down my throat like fizzy juice as I took swigs while walking down the street.

The club was a brick building on Wall Street, wedged between a drag bar and a tattoo parlor. With shaking hands, I smoked cigarette after cigarette across the street. It was dark inside — the windows were blacked out with paint. There was a large sign with the silhouette of a naked woman; her cartoon hair was the very same length as my own. I immediately felt more qualified. Next to her, the words DANCERS/MODELS WANTED were painted. The words, a simple request for application, promised a wholly different life. I had always admired women who were not ashamed of their sexuality, who had shed the guilt of their natural ability to seduce; and strippers were women who knew their sexual power, who used it and could make shitloads of money with it. They were hustlers, ghetto celebrities. Since leaving James, I had been wary of finding a new boyfriend. Meanwhile, I found myself consumed with sexual energy, a thirst that was never quenched by actual sex. Sex was rather crude, and I didn't trust anyone enough to press my body against theirs. Fantasy, just the thought of dancing, of teasing, seemed more satisfying somehow. *Then again.*

"I can't do this," I said aloud, and I walked away. I was half way to Mom's when the rotten sense of defeat caught up with me. I went to a payphone and called Elisa, hoping she would answer. Her parents still blamed me for her short stint away from home. When I heard her voice I sighed. "My best friend," I said. "I need advice."

I explained my dilemma, emphasizing the fact that "I really, really, really, need the money."

She said my voice was slurring and that I should contain myself. I became silent. "Look," she started in a firm, calm voice, "do you really want to be one of those girls no one wants?"

"I have no choice. I need to make some money," I said.

She sighed. "If it's what you feel you 'need' to do, go do it! First, go get another bottle of whatever it is you're drinking from Habib at the corner store and then get your ass in there, then show that ass to the world."

"Profound. Look, are you being sarcastic? I really don't think this is a bad thing,"

"Hey, I never said that!" Her voice was indignant.

"It's just that I think dancing is the quickest way to get money, to get on my own feet." I wanted to persuade her it was the right thing. I wanted her to encourage me.

"You don't have to tell me. Hell, I'd do it myself if I ever lost all this weight. You might as well go do this while you're still young. You still have the body and you'll look back on it and laugh when you're older and established."

"It'll be my jumping off point."

"Yeah, whatever," she said.

"Okay. I'm going to do it."

"Look, call me later and tell me what happened. I have to get back to studying." Elisa had already begun attending college, financed by her father. She had it easy, I thought.

I hung up and headed back toward the club. I decided to skip the extra bottle of wine, and take comfort from the cool, menthol smoke from my cigarette.

I also decided to walk past the club one more time, and on my way back, I'd go in. I tried to peek inside as I strolled by. There was a small part of the door that wasn't covered, but as I started to peek the door swung toward me. I straightened myself up and started on my way, thinking that I'd come back in a few months.

"Hey, you. Hey." I turned toward the voice. "You are a really pretty woman." The speaker was a kind-looking man in glasses and a golfer hat. I stared at him, wondering if he was a customer at the club. He wore khakis and a pressed polo shirt. I imagined he was someone's father, possibly someone's grandfather.

"Thank you," I started to move away again.

"Are you eighteen?"

"I will be in a month."

"You know, a girl as pretty as you could make a thousand dollars a week here." He stated this number as though numbers couldn't go any higher. For me, at the time, they didn't. He might as well have said a million.

I thought about prior jobs I'd had at Sam's Club and Bob Evans. I thought about the checks, the meager paychecks that didn't always cover my bills, let alone allow for me to save for college or a car. "That's a lot of money," I said, finally.

"We happen to be having open auditions today if you're interested. Can you dance?"

"I don't know if I can dance this way." I motioned to the silhouette.

He knew he had me. He extended a heavy muscular arm around my shoulder and walked toward the door. "There's no difference. You just dance. Come on, check out the club and then make your decision."

I left the sunny day behind me, and walked through a doorway leading to perpetual night. A short hallway with purple walls and an un-manned ticket window led to a large room with a lit stage at the center. There were two poles on the stage. A pretty blonde in jeans and shiny bra top was spraying them down with cleaner.

"Hey, Barry, who you got there?" she asked.

He nudged me, "None of us use our real names here. What name have you always liked?" I was confused and must have looked it because he looked me up and down and scratched his cheek, "This here is Georgia," he told the girl.

I blushed. "What?"

"Even if you don't end up working here, it's always good to have a stage name. You look like a girl I had a crush on in high school."

"Georgia! That's a pretty name. I haven't heard that one before. I'm Kelly. You here to audition?" She was smiling at me; her teeth were perfect and separated between two dimples. My teeth were not perfect. I smiled through closed lips.

"I don't even know how to audition," I said.

"Come over here." She curled a finger. I looked toward Barry and thought about running. He smiled warmly enough to block this impulse. I trusted him already.

Some very well-rehearsed coaxing later, I was up on the stage. I found myself walking slowly, around a pole that smelled of chemicals. I imitated Kelly who was showing me how to walk at an angle from the pole. I felt sloppy, like a Muppet, devoid of joints, raising heavy arms and legs around the stage. I flopped around, noticing myself in the numerous mirrors that lined the back half of the stage. I had always loved to dance and although I was delirious, awkward, I felt a strange sense of comfort on this stage. I was thinking about how natural dancing was, listening to a song I had never heard before, and I was almost lost in the rhythm when Kelly laughed suddenly. "That's it," she announced. She placed her long, slender fingers on my side, "Your hips are kind of big, but they'll go down quick, you'll see. Dancing every night sheds those pounds quickly."

"Don't listen to that anorexic bullshit," Barry demanded. "That's why I called you in here. That bottom half of yours is going to be a real money-maker. It makes you unique and beautiful." I blushed at the compliment. I felt silly thinking that my ass would be my namesake around here. After Kelly showed me her routine, I tried a version of it myself. After two songs, I sat down on the stage, winded from all the movement. My lungs were sore after so many cigarettes. Barry nodded, looked me over, and decided I had a place in the sexual, magnetic world of stripping.

"Are you out of shape?" he asked.

At the suggestion, I grew more determined. I got up and mimicked some of Kelly's "key moves," trying them again and again. I lifted my legs in the air, clinging to the pole and attempted to flip as she had. Kelly was patient with me, and showed me again and again until my Boones Farm buzz was long gone and I stopped, realizing that I was auditioning at a strip club. It's funny how reality slips away.

"This is a workout," I said, sitting cross-legged on the stage. *What the fuck am I doing?*

"Yeah, sure is, but you're a natural," Kelly said, "Do you dance?"

"I used to, if you count dancing in the living room every day after school throughout elementary school."

Kelly lit a joint casually as she spoke. "Are you going to work some tonight?"

"Huh? Do I have a job?"

"You're damn right you have a job. Stick around a few hours. You don't have to dance if you don't want to."

My stomach turned. "I don't think so," I said.

As if on cue, a man walked through the entrance. "Is there a charge to come in?"

"Twenty bucks," Barry said, his voice was deeper than before, and he began walking toward the man, his hand outstretched. The man paid.

Kelly leaned in toward me and whispered, "Watch and learn," and she disappeared behind the stage, leaving a trail of smoke behind her. I had never seen anyone smoke weed so casually.

I watched the man as he spoke to Barry. He wore a ball cap and suit. I thought the hat was either a reflection of bad taste or his attempt at anonymity. I wondered if he smelled the rich herbal smoke, if it bothered him, and if he recognized it. He sat down in front of the stage, and I walked behind him, toward Barry. My mouth felt dry, my hands were moist. I imagined myself trying to grab the pole on stage. I imagined my hands failing me, and my body flying across the stage as I tried to spin around; I imagined landing with a thud by this man's feet.

Kelly reemerged in a gorgeous shiny green skirt slit up to her hip, and a matching top. "You're here for the lunch special, sweetie?" she asked.

The man nodded. His hat matched the dark blue of his suit. I could see he was nervous and I wondered if this was his first time, too.

"Georgia," Barry called from his booth and motioned me toward the entranceway. His booth was small. Inside, Barry was moving dials and turning knobs, regulating the bass and volume of the song he was ready to play. He pulled a microphone from under the table. "Get ready," he said with a coy smile in my direction. Then he pulled the microphone close to his lips and lowered his voice. "Next up is the lovely...the sexy...our flirtiest blonde bombshell...the one, the only...Kelly!"

I watched from behind a window, staring up at stage. She emerged with glistening skin. The lights dimmed and the music began. A slow, steady techno beat filled the room. Kelly wore clear heels that lit up as she took each step. She stepped around the stage with confidence, pushing her curves from left to right, and all the while her eyes remained locked on the man in the cap. She was studying him as he studied her. She engaged him as though they were dancing together up there, and she was leading him.

The soft pink light made her body look flawless. Her face was almost indistinguishable, leaving only her precise makeup job visible. She was a complete fantasy. "She looks amazing," I said.

"So will you."

The first song faded and a ballad began, signaling Kelly to remove what appeared to be a sarong. Beneath her outfit was a matching bra and panty set with tassels hanging from the top. She waved them back and forth. The man waved dollar bills in turn. I felt their partnership established. They were equally exploited.

The man's hat lay by his side at the end of Kelly's dance. He threw dollar bills at her en masse as she executed her grand finale: a breathtaking series of flips and twirls that ended in mid-air splits.

"I can't do that," I said, pointing at Kelly whose legs straddled the air. Her arms were behind her, gymnastically suspending her flawless body.

"You don't have to," Barry said.

"I don't have an outfit."

"That skirt can be hiked up. Just lose the shirt." I looked down my own shirt. I had on a pretty black bra: silky, lacy. "Come on, Georgia, pick out a song."

"I need a drink."

Barry pulled out a flask and tilted it toward me. He was magical. As I drank he explained that girls usually did two songs up on stage but that he cut the songs short every time. If a customer wasn't throwing money, the songs would be only about a minute each.

"Even two minutes is a lot to improvise," I said.

"I'll just keep you up there for one song then."

"And stop it short?" I negotiated, thinking that this was only thirty or forty seconds of dancing. Barry watched as I gave in to the crippling capacity of my nervousness. I shook. The burning liquid seemed caught in my throat. I was used to wine and beer, but liquor was too harsh. At this moment, however, it seemed perfect. I took another sip and became liquid.

"I'll even cut it short if you feel uncomfortable, okay?" Barry asked. He smiled and turned a knob to lower Kelly's second song. "Now…a quick intermission and then a special treat," Barry announced, and flicked off the mike. "Drink up, sweetie," he said to me. "It's just rum."

I did. Next thing I knew, the announcement was for me, or for rather, Georgia, "And now we have a special treat," I heard Barry hum. "She's a virgin to our stage…please welcome the curvy, gorgeous redhead... Georgia."

I found myself walking toward the stage in heels that wobbled even though they were shorter than Kelly's. I walked myself behind the same entranceway Kelly had. I stepped slowly on the stage, making a smooth figure eight around the poles, just as I had been shown. I didn't hear the song Barry had picked for me, I couldn't listen to it, but somehow it flowed through me as the rum had, liquefying my body. So much so that I forgot that I was on stage to take off clothes. Kelly yelled up to me, "Take it off, sexy lady!"

These words hit me like a slap to the face. I looked down into the man's eyes, his eyes on my chest. I wondered why. I took my hand and followed his gaze with my fingers. I touched the buttons on my shirt; I undid them one at a time until my pretty black bra was exposed. I felt no shame. I felt the music. My hands continued to work, rolling the waist of my skirt, hiking it up, caressing my thigh.

I looked at him, realizing that *I* controlled his eyes now. The music grew louder and my movements became sharper. The man dangled a five dollar bill in the air and I bent close to him. He placed it in the strap of my bra. I rolled my skirt up another inch. I swung against the pole, sliding my back down it, opening my legs. The suited man was sweating. He mouthed some words that could have been "good job," but I looked away. I didn't want to know what he had to say.

The music softened. I bowed at the end of the song, rather stupidly, I thought. Then, I picked up my shirt. I hurried off the stage in a state of oh-my-God-what-have-I-done sort of exhilaration. I ran past Kelly, past the customer and directly to Barry's booth. "Can I have another sip of rum?"

"You drank it all."

"Shit."

"Georgia," Kelly sang. She appeared at the doorway. "The man out there wants a private dance from you. The dances are forty, eighty, or a hundred, depending on what kind of dance he wants. The hundred is five songs, the forty is one. Go see what he wants." She considered the scared look on my face. "Just tell him about the hundred first," she said, patting me on the shoulder. She grabbed my hand and led me toward him before I could run. My body seemed to loosen with her touch, hypnotically. Before I knew it we were next to the man and he no longer looked nervous. "Sit next to him and tell him you want to spend time with him."

I didn't want that much time. I didn't know that many moves, but my mind was reeling. The prospect of a hundred dollars for a few minutes of work began to sink in. I'm here for business, I told myself. I eased into the seat beside him. "I heard you want to spend some one-on-one time with me."

"I'd like that a lot."

"Well...you know I'm new, I don't know what I'm doing, but I think the hundred dollar dance is five songs and for forty dollars you get one song." I thought about selling Mary Kay. I thought about my last position, selling deodorizer. I remembered standing at the end of the cleaning aisle of a Sam's Club, flagging down customer after customer only to sell a grand total of one bottle. My manager told me my awful sale performance had broken even the lowest store record. She said I made history with my ineptitude. I promised I would improve, and I never went back.

"How many songs for eighty?" he asked.

"That's three songs," Kelly chimed in, "but Miss Georgia Peach here wants you for five."

He looked at me for verification but I just shrugged—bad sales technique. I didn't know what to do. I didn't want five songs. He handed me two crisp fifties from his wallet and Kelly smiled. She walked us back to an old plush couch. The man sat down, taking a seat in the middle of the couch and grinning.

I waited for Barry to begin the music. Kelly walked off. I watched, hoping she'd come back around. Then music grew louder. I heard the words this time. Wyclef Jean harmonized with The Neville Brothers. I thought of a mural on High Street I used to stare at as a kid. It was a recreation of Mona Lisa, angled and interpretively colored on the side of a condominium. I thought of Mount Pleasant, of my childhood home, of running away, being locked out, and then my thoughts went blank. I would dance many times after this, but I would never again have the reflective train of thought I had this day. I was still dancing. Throughout the duration of the song I maintained my distance while the man ogled. Maybe he thought it was something he was supposed to do, leaning in and widening his eyes, nodding as though his agreement kept me moving.

At the middle of the second song he asked me to get closer. I stepped between his legs and began to dance, bumping against him every now and then and backing away. "My name is Shawn," he said at the beginning of the third song. "This is funny, you know, I came here to get away from my life for a while, to be a man. And here you are, able to give me just that sort of service." He paused, watching me, waiting for a response. "How old are you, Georgia?"

"Twenty-one," I lied.

"You should be in college," he said. "Come, get closer."

My fourth song filled the room. "Have you ever had a private dance before?" I asked.

"A while ago."

"I think this is as close as I can get." I remembered Kelly's instructions and added, "Am I doing a good job for you, baby?" As I spoke, I heard my words as though someone else was saying them.

"You're perfection," he said. "It'd be even more perfect if you stepped on the couch and danced." I must have looked unsure. "That's what a couch dance is."

I did it. The rum was in my throat again, coming up. I heard loud voices and the tapping of heels behind me. "Put it on him, girl," I heard Kelly say. I heard another girl laugh, and I turned to watch them walk by. The other girl was heavyset. She was dressed in jeans and a polo shirt. She smiled, looked me up and down, and then I heard the two of them laugh again. I moved my foot around Shawn and my heel began to wobble in the couch. I fell into his lap like a pile of clothes, drunk.

"Sorry. Sorry. Sorry," I stammered as I stood up.

He laughed. "Do it again," he said. With his comment, the last song faded into the air. I apologized again and he handed me a twenty as a tip.

That wasn't so bad, I thought in the dressing room, staring at a cloudy mirror. Kelly and the other girl were back there, still laughing about people I didn't know. I was alone with my thoughts, watching my reflection, strangely proud. At the same time, I had had enough for the night. I felt as though my ability to face fears was exhausted. I sat in front of that mirror all night. When I was supposed to dance, I explained to the other girls that I was too dizzy to go onstage. When I was supposed to dance again, I said I was too sore. When I was to do my last dance, I said that I had to finish my cigarette then I disappeared into the bathroom and ignored the knock that came on the door and stared in that mirror. By the time the night ended, more bottles had appeared in the dressing room. I was too drunk to get out of my chair.

"Everyone gets drunk their first shift," Kelly said. "Most girls dance more than once, but you're good. You did damn good."

I collected my cash at the end of the night and as I counted it I noticed the same disconnected feeling I felt on stage. It was as though the money and the dancing were all part of some world that wasn't real to me. It was this surrealism I would cling to and begin a romantic relationship with. I asked the other girls how much they made, and determined that with income like this I'd have money for college in no time. "Right?" I asked Elisa. She said sure, it was easy. Money makes possibility, so now anything was possible. I would never avoid another dance. I would get there early and leave late.

Kelly introduced me around, new girls showed up for each shift, it seemed, for weeks, and at first I identified them by their dancing. It didn't take long to assimilate. Each day, girls arrived at all times in the late afternoon, making their way, one by one, into the dressing room for our ritualistic transformation. Glitter and powder designed to lighten or color, conceal or contour, was shared and traded, becoming community property in our dressing room. We took such care to exhibit our faces; girls, women: our faces were the focus in that dressing room yet they only ever earned a passing glance from customers as our bodies shifted and twisted onstage.

We knew that sexuality was expressed through the eyes and mouth, but our variety of salesmanship was less nuanced; our product was vulnerability, nakedness, false promise of sexual conquest. Yet, we spent hours in front of the mirrors smoking, doing lines, gossiping, speculating, all while constructing our masks with care and precision.

Falling (off stage)

When people ask me why I stripped, I go with the simple answer: I was curious and confused. In many ways, I still am. Yes, I *did* want to go to college and I *was* poor, but I had a more nuanced, less sociological reason for sauntering past that strip club in my short gray skirt. I can't claim low self-esteem or sexual oppression. It wasn't daddy issues or the rise of the MTV culture—I never even had cable! In fact, I made my decision in part because dancing seemed thrilling to me, and glamorous in much the same way running away had been.

A decade ago, I had the desire to be looked at, defined and redefined—even criticized, so long as I was seen. Even then, I was a living story, begging to be read. Now, I write about my life, my innermost thoughts. The desire for exposure seems constant in my life. But, had I known what stripping would be like, I'd have picked up the pen much earlier.

***

I remember sitting on a blanket-covered couch with another blanket across my lap, picking at a bacon and egg sandwich. I was calling off of work, figuring that girls would have to miss at least one or two days each month.

"I'll be back in a couple of days," I said.

"Just cut the string," Terri said through a knowing laugh. And, just like that, stripping became a real job. It required me to clock in, ready or not, in order to get paid.

After two months, I felt I had earned my stilettos. If someone were to stop me in the street to check my bag here is what they would have found: body glitter, three or four outfits, makeup, a small flask of liquor, and maybe cigarettes. I often quit and started back up. I found myself in a comfortable routine: waking up at three, walking the six blocks to work in sweats or jeans and my shiny black stilettos at four, drinking my dinner with Barry, and then spending a few cigarettes, or a few cigarettes worth of time, slathering myself with the glitter and makeup before we opened the club. Dinner consisted of a fifth of corner store Long Island Iced Tea which would get me through the first few hours, and then I would take a break around midnight and go to the bar next door and order a Tequila Sunrise, or three. The liquor in my flask was for after the bar closed, or in the event that the bar denied me service.

The owner of the bar knew my age and had banned me repeatedly, but I always tried. The days he was not there I tipped well, so many of the bartenders ignored the rules. To add to the bartender's peace of mind, I always ordered a soda that I kept next to my drink, in case the owner stopped in unannounced.

I had perfected the dance by this time. I had fun with it, flipping and doing backbends on stage. I stretched and practiced at home. There was a definite sexuality in the act of taking my clothes off, and a feeling of sexiness—but more than anything, stripping was a business. Some girls loved the job. Some girls were turned on by the power of the dance, the undivided attention. I didn't exactly become turned on, but I was empowered, and I got lost in the mystery of dance: its freedom of movement and rhythm; its ability to maintain attention, to communicate to the audience. I expressed myself on stage and felt my femininity rise from a stifled place inside me. My dancing became almost a form of meditation. Until, that is, I looked down at the equally meditative glances from below. The audiences sickened me. Many of the girls said they felt the same way. Ebony told me, "You'll hate men after doing this for a while." And, on occasion, I did.

I began to drink more, but no matter how drunk I got, the customers never went away. They were just men (and occasionally women) who flicked their dollars at the stage, or stuffed the bills in my bra-top, my bottoms. I learned to watch for the mannerisms of grabbers or those who tried to proposition me. Hatred and fear stung my ear as I heard the words "take it off," as I bared my ass. I heard over and over again that the classier strip bars only required a woman to bare her breasts. We were the dregs, the low-class girls who showed everything in exchange for a higher price point, a lower class of clientele.

I had to find a sort of mental freedom from this job, I remember thinking. I would have to make my reality silly, something to play with. This would get me through. I would dance, naked, but I would always be more than a girl dancing. I would be shaping a future in my mind, planning my success, ignoring the moments that hurt. The glamour was gone, but I could still construct a place to hide, inside a future that didn't include this life, only looked back knowingly upon it. I tried my best to perfect my on-stage meditation; not let the customers in. Some days it worked.

I had lost ten pounds. My cheeks looked as though they were caving in. Although I was a small person, I was obviously not meant to be just over one hundred pounds; Elisa explained this repeatedly as we sat in my mother's living room with coffees on the rug beside us. We were rummaging through my makeup, which was quite a collection, and I was offering her various lipsticks and eye shadows that I thought were too harsh for my complexion. "You know, I am making less money than I was when I started," I said.

This sealed Elisa's theory that men like curves, not bones. "There you have it. You know, maybe it would help if you didn't smell like a distillery. Girl, you are always drunk lately."

"Whatever," I said. I had managed to party almost every night, buy some of the most expensive dancing outfits imaginable, and still save twelve hundred dollars. This was more than enough to move out of my mom's house, so I had to keep going.

"Does Miss Sarah have her pink Cadillac yet?" I asked, eager to talk about something else.

"Uh, no. I don't think she's even selling Mary Kay right now. She said something about taking a sabbatical from her career. Mom's crazy."

"I miss your mom."

"She hates you, you know." Elisa was always honest.

"I know."

Elisa had been asking to come see the club since I began dancing. So we walked there together and I introduced her to Barry. The two got into a conversation about chess and promised each other a game some time soon. Self-righteously, I said that I could beat them both, but they ignored me. Dad and I used to play chess, and he had shown me how to take my time, consider the entire board. "That's why I beat you Jen, your snap decisions." I had also played with James, whom I would usually beat, and Mr. Emer, who gave me strategic advice: "Always play black. Most will start with white to E4. Don't mirror that move; always counter with C3 or C5 then knight to C6." I don't recall ever beating Mr. Emer.

I walked toward the stage. Kelly was there. Kelly was always there. And she began to flip, impressing Elisa with her moves the same way she had done for me months ago. Elisa giggled and ran up to the stage to twirl around the poles.

"You all should have more big girls working here. You skinny girls have nothing to shake," she said from the stage. Barry responded by playing a rap song that called her to gyrate. Elisa did. She bounced her breasts and then her butt. She never stopped giggling.

When we opened the club, Elisa sat in the back of the room and watched me dance. Afterward she said she was impressed that I had become so acrobatic. I thanked her. It felt strange to have her there, have two pieces of my life touch. When she finally left, after making small talk with some of the dancers, I was relieved.

***

Stripping is tough. I could probably still do it, but I doubt I would sustain the level of physical dedication I had then, the desire to get the most customer requests. I had to work twice as hard, Kelly once told me, due to *my* major flaw: small breasts. A woman, small-breasted or no, who makes her living as a dancer in the Midwest must be consistent in order to stockpile those thousands that she is promised in local newspaper ads.

There were six regular girls who worked the club: Diamond, a small girl with a big coke habit; Glitter, a beautiful girl with a day job and a part-time college career; Kelly, my mentor and at age thirty-two the oldest stripper at the club; and Candi. She was beautiful until you got too close, her face covered in scars. Candi was a muscular girl who could make it to the stripper Olympics with the tricks she could do on the poles. Finally, there was Terri, a heavy girl who had a niche following and cried about her weight daily. I was the redhead.

Barry had truly taken to me. It was in no way a sexual relationship, but definitely a close one. For this reason, I got away with everything. He would cut my songs short when I wanted him to, make sure I had the lighting perfect, and pledge to safeguard me from any menacing customer. Other girls would roll their eyes at our beginning to play chess when the club was slow. He almost always beat me. When he first met me, Barry confided that he didn't think I would fit in at the club—he thought that I wouldn't last, or maybe shouldn't, and that I should be like Glitter and go back to school. "Just do this a while," he suggested, "then try school." Later, I would question his sincerity.

While Barry and I bonded, I kept my distance from most of the other girls. Terri was my drinking partner and confidante, and Kelly had no real opinion of me that I could discern. She always seemed upbeat. But both Glitter and Diamond hated me out of competitiveness and they spread rumors that Barry and I were sleeping together and that I was a lush. Okay, so they had one out of two.

One day, they joined me at the bar and said we should all do shots together. I thought they were finally accepting me, that I had misjudged them. They were finally letting me in to their group. Glitter said she would take care of the first round.

The shots went down my throat like fire. I needed a mixer. I remembered vaguely how drunk I got the first day I danced, and I thought I should slow down. I thought of this too late. I was already drunk. Kelly came over to the bar and asked the bartender for a soda water to take next door.

"You want a shot?" I slurred.

Glitter smacked her lips and mumbled something to Diamond before tapping off in her stilettos, toward the bathroom.

"I can't drink, sweetie," Kelly said, smiling at the bartender as he set down a glass with lime.

"Why not?"

"I have hepatitis." She said this flatly.

I didn't know what this was, exactly. I put my drink down. "Is that an STD? What does that have to do with drinking?"

"No," she said. "You can get it from needles. I used when I was in Vegas. No big deal, everyone did." Kelly always talked about being a showgirl in Las Vegas. She seemed to miss her life there.

"I want to go to Vegas," I said. "I want to get out of Ohio."

Kelly shook her head, as though there was no chance in hell. She then laughed warmly and called out to the rest of the girls. "Come on, girls, we have to get back over there. Barry asked me to get you all."

Just as she said this, Barry appeared in the doorway, hollering. "A bunch of young guys just came in. Get your asses over there. Break's over."

"Aw, man," I said. Young guys rarely tipped more than a few dollars; they were poor. It was the old, married, guilty-looking men who tipped best, the ones who opened their wallets as though they had to pay you off, without salacious comments or advances. I wonder: Otherwise, did they think I would follow them home, tell their wife, or show up at their church and whisper something in the deacon's ear as they sat there red-faced and raw? Or could it be that an older man, with more perspective on the world at large, had genuine respect for us, in our position, just doing our jobs?

We hustled over to the club and walked around the back to the dressing room. There, I realized that my wallet was missing. "You'll have to go on first," I told Kelly. "I can't find my wallet."

"Sure thing, sweetie."

I ran back over to the bar and looked around for my wallet. Nothing. I checked with the bartenders, in the bathrooms, and below the bar. I was still searching, when Barry showed up again. "What's going on? The customers seem bored, they need the redhead."

I looked at him, trying to portray my panic. "Someone stole my wallet," I said. "Where's Glitter?" I was thinking that Glitter disappeared early, she had been nice to me, had bought my shots. Glitter had stolen my wallet, I was sure of it. "Where's Glitter?"

"She left. She said she had to go somewhere real quick and would be back. That's why we need you over there," Barry motioned toward the club as he began to back out of the door.

"She left? I knew it! She stole my fucking wallet!"

"Come on back over, Georgia. Dance and we'll get to the bottom of this later. Glitter probably didn't steal it. It's probably just at the club somewhere."

"That bitch has my wallet," I said. My rage was sobering.

Barry put his arm around me and walked me out of the bar. "Don't worry," he murmured. He walked me to the DJ booth and handed me his flask. I drank its contents as though it were ice water. "Listen, sweetie. Just go up there for a song. These college guys are being dicks, not really tipping, so I'll cut your songs real short."

"Okay, just give me a minute," I said, as we walked in. I continued walking, past Barry's DJ station, past the rows of jeans and baseball caps, past Kelly who was now giving a couch dance to a college kid with big ears. I walked into the dressing room. I covered myself with shimmer lotion and applied thick blue eyeliner and smothered my lips with pink gloss. I could see myself wavering in the mirror and steadied my chin with my hand. Maybe I was still drunk.

Terri stroked my back. "Georgia, come on. Barry is announcing you next. You have to get out there." I hadn't heard.

I swallowed hard and said something about Glitter and my wallet, then rested my head against the counter. I don't remember how, but the next thing I knew, I was up on the stage with Wyclef Jean and the Neville Brothers singing to me, guiding my body softly around the stage, soothing my ears, flowing alongside the drink that consumed my body. I was swaying from pole to pole. From the stage I skipped upward to do my standard routine flip between the poles. I was up, and the next thing I knew I was falling. I don't know how my hand loosened from the pole, but I hit the stage on my hands and my legs floundered down afterward, following gravity's direction, pulling my body off the stage and toward the floor beneath. I landed, somehow, on my feet, wobbling against a customer as I began to stand, but my hand was bent back and stuck on stage. I pulled it toward me and felt a tug hold me there.

The man I landed next to handed me a dollar and did not smile or say anything. He nodded to my hand and I noticed the blood. A small nail sticking out from the stage had stopped my hand on the way down, and tore open my palm, a half-inch tear that released disturbing amounts of blood. I apologized to one of the men, loosened my palm from the nail, and fell backwards into a chair.

Terri walked me home. I was fading in and out of reality as I leaned against her shoulder. I couldn't walk in to Mom's apartment so bloody and drunk I remember thinking, quite astutely. I woke the next day to my pager buzzing between my hip and the concrete below. I had been sleeping in a small alcove behind a church next to the apartment. I hid there until she left for work. I made a fist, cracking a clay-colored coat of flaky blood. The injury didn't look as bad as I had remembered. It was a deep but small tear, a crescent moon, beneath my index finger. Now, it's white, hardly detectable.

When I managed to get in the apartment the first thing I did was check the clock: ten. I called Terri.

"Glitter said she was going to kick your ass," Terri warned. "I wouldn't go in to work today if I were you."

"Glitter is anorexic. I could blow and she'd fall over," I said. "Besides, she is the one that robbed me, not the other way around."

"You're not looking too voluptuous yourself anymore," Terri said.

"I can take her," I assured.

"Yeah, but she's crazy. Besides, are you sure she stole your wallet?"

"Yes. And because everything I had was in it, I really need the money, Terri. I just spent most everything on a down payment for an apartment and I still need to buy furniture and glassware, and a hundred other miscellaneous things that people need to live. I move in soon. You know I had over two hundred dollars in that wallet?"

I hadn't actually signed the lease yet, but I had found a nice little apartment close to my mom's. It was small, but still within walking distance of the club. I had no intention of getting a driver's license, so walking distance was crucial. I leaned the phone against my ear as I cleaned the remaining dried blood from my hand. I found some butterfly bandages in Mom's bathroom and doctored my wound with hydrogen peroxide.

Terri sighed at the other end. "Georgia, I worry about you," she said. I supposed that was why some of the girls called her Mom. I assured her that I would be fine. She sighed again before saying she'd see me at work.

Family consumed my mind as I rested. What would Mom think? She was worried about me at this time, but I figured she was okay; she continued to move forward, upward, getting small raises at work and paying her bills each month. I helped her out, but she often refused my money.

How was my sister doing? She had moved out by this time, and I rarely saw her. My family had become a series of faded slides in my mind, rotating and waking me up this day, and then comforting me back to sleep. It was my father, finally, and a feeling that there was something broken between us, a flash of discontent that woke me up for good. I knew that when I got my own place, things would be different. He could visit on my terms. And, instead of constantly being reminded of my mistakes, from running away to worrying my mother, I could take comfort in the fact that I wasn't affecting anyone but myself.

I knew I was bad for Mom. I also knew that living with her only fed my resentment toward Dad. If I moved out, I'd only be responsible for me. In the meantime, I couldn't let any bitch get away with delaying my plan. James had taught me not to let anyone bully me, and he was right. Glitter had stolen far more from me than two hundred dollars, and I had no choice but to fight her.

The Turn-around

It was 1998. As I lay on Mom's patchwork couch, my hand throbbing, my anger stewing, I resolved to get hydrated and make it to work. In a way, it is possible that the volatile life I was living—alcohol, dancing, fighting—fixed my anxiety or distracted me from my depressed thoughts, those that have only decided to emerge when my life calmed down. The lifestyle I had then just did not allow for petty depression and self-loathing. Sure, I was around danger, but I couldn't allow myself to be intimidated. I was tough. I could take on Glitter.

***

Glitter didn't show up at work until late in the shift, and by that time the evidence only further supported my case against her. My wallet, now empty, had surfaced. So, bolstered by too many drinks, I confronted her as soon as I saw her. I accused her. An outright accusation caught everyone in the club off guard. Time seemed to slow down and the room became still. Glitter dialed a number into her phone, and asked me what the fuck I was thinking.

Her ferocity interested me. Her beauty was wrinkled and twisted into waves of sheer hatred; I could feel the callousness of her stare rising on my skin. She looked like she wanted to kill me, but chose instead to play things a bit more practical and yell.

"You think it was me?"

"Hell, yes, I do. Lena found my ID behind the women's toilet last night. That ID came from my wallet. We were the only people left in the whole damn bar, and I know Terri wouldn't do it."

"No one calls me a thief. Don't you understand that I'm the one bitch here that's doing something with her life? Why would I steal from you?" She was referring to her part-time enrollment in community college, I supposed, which was hardly impressive to me—seeing as how I, too, planned to go back to school.

"You would steal from me because you're jealous. I make more money here." She glared. There was a moment of silence between us in which we became stuck in each other's eyes. One of us would have to either speak or move. I took the cue. "You're a goddamn thief."

Barry yelled something toward us, something to the effect of "Calm down!"

But Glitter's voice was gaining conviction. "No one, you hear me, calls me a thief!" She wore a teal dress that shimmered, accented by a white boa around her shoulders. She looked like a drag queen. And then her face changed. She smiled suddenly and I found this odd. Maybe she was planning to redeem herself and give me back my money? If so, we would be friends again. I wasn't one to hold grudges. A noise distracted me.

I turned around. A big, monstrous-looking girl was moving toward us, eyes fixed on me. "Don't accuse my sister of anything unless you can back it up with proof."

"I don't even know you," I said. "What do you have to do with this?" I was about to add something else, something quick-witted I'm sure, when two beefy hands pushed me around and up against a wall. I felt a sharp sting at the back of my head. My forehead hit the wall and rebounded from it sharply. I yelled for her to get off of me, feeling my body shrinking toward the ground. My balance eluded me. I felt as though I was desperately trying to tread air like water, pushing at it while gravity's response could only pull me down quicker. My arms were up like a boxer, protecting my head, and I could feel her sloppy, heavy punches thrash at my sides. I felt the floor, sticky and gritty. I felt no pain, only dissolution. Then, suddenly, they stopped.

Barry was peeling the girl off of me. Glitter yelled, "Why are you always defending this uppity bitch? It's fucked up, Barry."

I charged toward Glitter. The monster lunged again. Barry wedged his way between us all, blocking us with his body.

I wiped blood from my eyes and realized I was dizzy. I worked diligently at my balance now, thinking, for some reason, about how this moment, this one tiny piece of time was moving slowly as those that Buddhists say are achieved through mediation.

The taste of honey filled the back of my throat. I could barely see the bar, make out the outline of Barry, his body blocking me from the girl. Something made a *CRACK*. I looked through the redness collecting around my eyes. I heard muffled voices and wiped the blood from my face. The brutish girl had broken free from Barry's grasp and was trying to move around him, trying to get at me. Barry's fist was recoiling from her forehead, and there in the center of her monstrous face, a zigzag split was working its way from her hairline down to the bridge of her nose. She looked as bad as I felt. Barry had knocked the monstrosity right out of her.

Lena, the bartender began wrapping ice in a towel. I wondered who she was going to hand it to, and suddenly that became all that mattered. I lost the battle, I thought, but I was going to be damned if this bitch would get the ice handed to her first. I wedged in between her and the barstool next to her, watching her disbelief from this close distance as I thrust my hand out for the wrapped ice. Lena handed it to me.

It dawned on me now that the girl who just pummeled my face was inches from me. I could have danced on her head and she would not have noticed. I stared at her, ready to ask why, when a hand squeezed and pulled at my shoulder. "Come on, girl," Terri pulled me toward the back entrance and out into the frigid night air. She was frantic, fussing over my broken face as gently as my mother would have.

From outside, I could hear Glitter screaming, "Why?" at Barry.

I watched him walk toward the entrance of the club, telling Glitter to go home, to sleep it off.

"I'm not coming back, Barry!" I said it with a pout in my voice that surprised me.

He turned. "Maybe that's good," he said, and angled his golfer hat to its precise position on his head.

My heart began to pound against my ribs. This girl would come after me again. But her face was pudgy and childlike, fat around the cheeks. My last dance, I figured. This was the third fight I had been in. The third one I'd lost. I wanted to give her my ice pack, tell her I was sorry. I wondered if she needed to go to the hospital.

I moved beyond Barry, who was now lighting a cigarette and told him goodbye. I'm sorry, Barry. I just have to leave. I don't feel good about all this."

He pulled out a flask, but I shook my head and brushed past him. One of the heels on my shoes had broken off. I was a ghetto Cinderella, hobbling back toward the pumpkin after getting the shit kicked out of me. I took both shoes off and threw them toward the bus stop from the door.

I walked away. From outside, I could hear the girl, Mica that is, come back to life. Maybe she had just been stunned. She began screaming from the ambulance, "I'm going to fucking kill her! You better watch out, Barry. All of you better watch out. I'm going to get my cousins and shoot your goddamn club up."

***

Irony isn't always funny, though it is often noteworthy. While I was hung over on the couch, out of touch with reality, my mother worked at a drug and alcohol treatment center on the west side of town. I was an addict, and Mom knew more than I thought she did. She had a gift for relating to addicts where she worked; people sought her out, confided in her while her own daughter stumbled in the apartment at four in the morning. All she could do was place a blanket over my body and make sure that there was food in the fridge, if I ever needed it. She was waiting me out, clinging to the faith that I would come around on my own. There was more predictability to my behavior than I knew.

Mom's father had been an alcoholic. My grandfather drank enough liquor in his lifetime to literally drown in the stuff. He was so devoted to drinking that he couldn't waste time, those few extra years, it would've taken for cirrhosis to set in and take him out at a slightly older age. By the time he died, he had abandoned Mom, left her to live with her mother, who continued to binge drink until she crashed her car into a storefront. Embarrassment somehow overshadowed her desire to drink from then on.

When my parents split, there was no drinking involved. Perhaps this is what hurt Mom the most, being left by a sober man. Dad was in the midst of his "renaissance period." And when Mom told me about their plans to split, relief had trumped any remorse I may have otherwise felt because I knew she was miserable and yet never would have left him. Family was supposed to be uncomfortable for her, it seemed, because it always had been. I would find this out much, much later.

My drinking was nothing new to Mom, nor were broken relationships—her father had left his family before he drowned. He had remarried before bothering to divorce my grandmother and they no longer heard from him. She had a lifetime of training; she was adept at dealing with abandonment, drunkards. I remember worrying about her for the wrong reasons. I remember going to a meeting with her when I was a kid, sitting in those foldable chairs in a smoky room, listening, trying to make up stories.

The Last Dance

Unfortunately, that bit about the fight wasn't the pinnacle of my stripping career. In fact, I went back to work where I stewed in my cocktails and quick money. Glitter wasn't there. Nor was she there the next day, or the next. Even now, I don't know that it would do any good to go into a logical analysis that justifies my decision to go back. My current perspective, years of therapy and reassessment, all tell me that I was still clinging to the fantasy that I could make this lifestyle work. To really get inside my head then, however, I recall thinking something more akin to, hey, I like the job, I'm paid well, dancing replaces pesky sexual desires I might otherwise have, and the position comes with flexible hours and a generous on-the-job drinking allowance.

Besides, I rarely entertained the notion that Glitter and Mica would actually have the club shot up. Such threats didn't seem realistic to me. Who would care to shot up a strip club because two dancers tussled?

Perhaps I didn't really fear guns. I had seen plenty of them, some up close, and they were always just for show and threat. One day after high school, Damien, the bully, that guy that stole my Walkman and beat on women, had flashed a gun at me as a joke then got angry when I didn't cower. Another time, Barry showed me that I had nothing to worry about if a customer put his hands on me, showing me he kept a .44 Magnum by the door. James's father kept a rifle in his house, unloaded. James had once shown me the shoebox where his father kept the bullets; he'd said they were over ten years old but could still kill. But these were just words.

Despite close proximity to firearms, I never considered guns intimidating; instead, they seemed to me a mode of protection. I might as well have been a card carrying member of the NRA. Guns, to me, were an accessory, a symbol of fearlessness and control in dire situations. That was my thinking until bullets were flying right outside the club, possibly directed at me.

***

I didn't recognize the sound as shots, but I heard a succession of blasts. They seemed close, whizzing by, just outside the dressing room where I sat applying makeup with a shaky hand. It had been weeks since my fight. I was in the dressing room nursing a bottle of strawberry wine, a low proof; the ethanol was taking too long to reach my bloodstream. The shots seemed to exacerbate the way my body quivered, so I reached for a fresh pack of cigarettes. I was glad to have the extra time to prepare this day, but it was getting late; I couldn't help but wonder why my regulars hadn't arrived for the early dances. One of these gentlemen was elderly, a sweet man, really, with a thing for redheads. He tipped low, but our exchange was predictably easy: he would get a couch dance, asking that I play a slow song, so that he could keep up with my dancing. He never spoke much, and I often used these minutes to think of practical things, such as what I would need from the grocery store the next day, or whether I had saved enough money to sign up for a psychology or sociology class here and there at the community college.

The other regular, whose name or alias I don't recall, was nowhere near as predictable an experience. He was a tall, muscular Jamaican man, with inviting milky brown eyes that never left my own. He liked to mix things up, sometimes opting for the couch or the private room. Mostly, though, he would pay for a few songs so that we could just talk in private, with me near naked, of course. He seemed eager to believe that I was going to quit the club soon and run off with him. I would have promised him anything, the way he threw money my way, usually tipping fifty just for the talk. We would discuss my plans for the future and his work as a DJ at a nearby reggae club. He was the sort of man who made me forget where I was, and, had I met him anywhere else, I probably would have been the one pursuing him.

"Monica," he held my gaze as he pronounced the name I had told him I used outside of the club, "You, my dear, do not belong here. You don't look natural here. You stand out, but you won't always. You have to leave this place."

"You don't belong here, either," I told him. "Why are you here, if you think so little of the place?"

"My first time, for a buddy. Ever since, for you." He told me I would love Jamaica, in his neighborhood, which was safe and mostly free of crime, where neighbors would sit out all day on their porches telling each other stories and smoking the best ganja in the world. He told me other, more disturbing things about the island, reasons he'd left. "It is illegal to be gay there, you know," he told me, at ten dollars a minute, "And you would never want to go there alone, as a tourist. White women, especially older ones, go there for anonymous sex, and so it is expected. There is a lot of HIV and AIDS, lots of dirty happenings."

I often fought the urge to invite this man out for coffee, but lately he had begun bringing me presents, which erased this urge from my mind. Presents brought to the club were a bad sign, the sign of a stalker. And when he presented me with a ring box, I was warned to stop talking to him so much. I had opened the box with a soft, warm feeling in my belly. It was a gold ring with my alias's initial on it; a row of diamond chips lined the last line of the M. At the time, I didn't think to give so personal a gift back to him, and I was shocked to see that it fit my finger, size 5 ¾; how could he have known?

As I thought about this man, frantically searching my memory for his name, I gazed down at the ring, which I always wore at the club now. It was often flashed as proof when customers questioned whether my real name was Monica. When I walked past the heavy burgundy curtain and onto the club floor, I was shocked to see that it was virtually empty— unheard of on a weekend. Then a new girl, Honey, ran in hollering about what had happened.

"I almost stepped right over him." She bent over to catch her breath, and then looked behind her as though she were being chased.

"Calm down, sweetie. Let's go back to the back. Tell me what you saw."

"Fuck. Okay. You have a cigarette?" I packed her a Newport and lit it, passing it to her carefully. She shook more than I did, which meant I was in control here.

"Honey?"

"Okay, so I stepped over this guy, right? I thought he was just passed out. Then the police appeared out of nowhere and started putting up their yellow tape. I don't know who he was, but no one can really tell for sure because his face is blown off." All the girls at the club, who had gathered around, were still. She took a breath and went on. "He was coming over here, I think. No one remembered seeing him at the bar or anything." I took a swig of my wine, not really considering the fact that what she was saying could be decoded to mean a man was dead only a few dozen feet from where I was sitting. Remarkably, I noticed then, I had stopped shaking.

As Honey told her story, I decided I would spend the night right where I was. I was not dancing for anyone, and I had enough wine to last me a while. Another girl had entered the club as she spoke, claiming to have lost her hearing in one ear due to the proximity of the shots. Blue uniformed officers entered our club successively for the next hour, questioning each of us about what we had heard, seen, and when. One rather familiar officer—whom usually we detested seeing since he would cause a frenzy of girls rushing to bury bags of coke in the floorboards— filled us in on the gritty details.

According to the witnesses, a man had been shot in the face by another. The shooter lingered for a moment, spewing profanities at the writhing body, and then jumped in a vehicle and sped off. I didn't fear those with vengeance on their mind, but this man seemed insane to me. Most shooters go for the heart. The face is messy, inviting the physical chaos of flying bone fragments and the possibility the victim will live. They thought the gun had been a .38 caliber, a large caliber bullet that had moved at a slow enough velocity to knock the man down instead of going directly through his skull. The bullet was probably lodged somewhere below the muddled mess of tissue and blood that buried his face. At the time, despite a currently horrified narrator, I remember actually wanting to see the man's face, but luckily no one volunteered to go with me.

The waves of whoops from more police cars caused us to huddle around and speculate about the crime. Barry had thought the two men had been brothers, the victim caught with the shooter's wife. I thought they had just gotten into a street brawl, some gang shit, or some crazy who just wanted to see the power of his own trigger finger. Our stories alone made the whole thing seem like fiction, even though our soundtrack was a cacophony of cries and sirens. We all stayed quiet inside as the night progressed; no one wanted to leave until Barry ventured outside. He announced that the area was clear and we should pack up our things.

The club closed down early that night, and most of the girls went home. Barry said he was going to a bar, and Terri and I tagged along. Now that I was outside of the club, I was afraid to go home. What if that guy was one of my regulars, I wondered, and the other had been a wife's sister's husband who was sent to kill me but killed him instead? My drunken inventiveness was in high gear. "Where they after me?" I asked stupidly.

I had finished my bottle of wine quickly and been passed a flask at some point in the night, which I'd kept close to my lips at all times, never giving it back to the bouncer that handed it to me. My question would bring the first genuine chuckle I'd heard in hours, and, as the night progressed; if there was a moment of silence someone would mock me, repeating my question in a high-pitched, childlike voice. The laughter became more voracious as I still entertained notions of fantastical self-centered violence. I had silently begun to believe that this whole incident had been somehow connected to my fight with Glitter, and such narcissism fed my thirst and allowed me to ignore the banter.

Barry bought the bar a round, dedicated to me. "To Georgia, our little gangster," he said.

Later, the night turned. Last call was approaching and we had to drink quickly. After a few shots, our fear was replaced with pure liquor-induced insights. We began discussing spirituality, as drunks do—vociferously.

I began quoting some book on Zen, something about living in the moment and how impossible that was for people in threatening surroundings. Terri said she didn't understand what I meant. I downed a shot and got sidetracked, so I didn't press the issue.

I noticed a couple of guys who had been at the club earlier that evening. They had thrown twenties and fifties at the stage all night, spending at least a thousand dollars before they left. They were the reason I had almost six hundred dollars tucked away after only an hour of work. The tall one had bought a four-song couch dance from me and then tipped me a hundred dollars. Meanwhile, the short one had spent a lot of time trying to get my phone number. He said that he knew I was smart and he wanted to make me his girlfriend. I almost laughed, because I heard this as a joke from some of the friendly, taunting regulars and as a serious proposal from some of the creepier, disillusioned sort, but when I saw that he seemed to mean everything he was saying, I backed away from him. He had a strange sort of seriousness for someone his age.

As dancers, we made a collective pact to never date customers, and never give out phone numbers. There was something about being on stage that made certain men look at you as a challenge. Such men wanted to save you from yourself and set you on the right track, as though you were a community service project for them to take on. He seemed like the type, I thought. He wore his uniform and sat up straight, scrutinizing my body with subtle appreciation. He was studying me.

When they walked over in the bar and offered to buy us a round, I accepted. Barry smacked me on the arm and gave me the "you know better" look that I knew all too well. After another drink and some conversation, however, Barry had let down his guard. The tall one was named Sid and said he was only home for another day. He was in the Army Reserves. He talked about the training, which gained Barry's favor because of his own history in the military.

The short one was named Derek. Eventually he accepted my lack of interest and instead revived the topic of religion. Terri asked him, voice wavering with drink, what he thought. His response angered her. He said all people are agnostic and those who say they are not are only taking a specific position on creation so that they can feel superior to others. Terri said that Christianity made sense to her because it was about loving others, not feeling superior. Derek asked why there were so many interpretations of the same religion, then.

She said, "To assume we are all agnostic is not only self-righteous and superior in of itself, it is also blasphemous." She said that atheists and agnostics all thought themselves to be superior, but they were really just confused.

"I think I'm agnostic," I said. "But I don't know for sure."

Derek laughed. "On to other things," he said. "Vodka is superior to rum. Rum is for girls." He pointed at Terri's rum and coke. He was drinking straight vodka now.

"You're full of shit," she said. "Rum is the best of sugary liquors that exists."

"You are both correct," I said, standing. I ordered one of each and sat back, astonished at the shift of conversation. That was when I realized I was drunk—a difficult feat for someone with my tolerance, I thought.

Neither Sid nor Derek had heard about what happened at the club, and when we told them they got a little more sober. Barry bought us all shots of something that was lit on fire then plunked into a full beer that we had to chug. It tasted like cola and I immediately wanted another one. Derek insisted on buying one for me, and I insisted on lighting the shot myself. I pulled out a Zippo lighter and coolly turned back the top, lit a flame and held it to my shot. Derek held my beer right underneath it, so that I could plunk it right in. When the shot caught flame, it turned blue and orange so quickly that I immediately wanted to drop it. I did and Derek caught it in the beer. Then he pointed to my arm. A small yellow flame was creeping up my arm and as soon as I looked at it, it was gone. My light arm hair was singed and my skin felt tingly and light. Now I had proof. I was drunk.

Derek told me to go the bathroom and run my arm under cold water. Terri went with me, and we hovered over my singed arm, wondering why it didn't look any different.

"I think your arm hair is completely gone, but you can't really tell a difference," she said pulling my other arm to compare. "You are ridiculous, Georgia. Just ridiculous."

"Yeah," I agreed and pulled my bag up to the mirror. Then we took our time applying makeup and giggling about how the military men were too serious, but actually kind of cute. We stumbled back out the door with the same goal: to sustain our drunkenness. Derek was waiting for us by the pool tables with two new shots and a red lighter in hand, a big smile on his face.

"Where's Barry?" I asked Terri.

She pointed to the end of the bar where he sat, head tilted down. I had never seen Barry so drunk as that night. He didn't even say goodbye. He may have forgotten where he was. I watched in disbelief as he practically fell out the door and into a yellow cab. He had asked me if I wanted to share a cab earlier that night, but I had refused. Still, I thought he would have said goodbye. I was too drunk to stop drinking now, I thought. Something propelled me away from the conscious world. I wanted more of what I felt. The guys were standing around us, encircling us—they were offering to take us home, saying they were not drunk, but I insisted we go to an after-hours spot down the street where we could continue to drink until six in the morning. I wanted to play poker, too.

We went. The after-hours was a small house run by an elderly black woman named Mrs. Jackson who wore a scarf around her thick gray hair. She had a bar in the living room and charged us each ten dollars to play poker with her and a few men and women who were much less drunk than we were. I apologized for Terri, who ended up passing out as soon as we walked through the door. I paid her way just so that she could sleep on the couch.

***

Derek, Sid, and I continued to play poker and drink until Mrs. Jackson announced the last game. She said she had to close. Here is where things began to go downhill. Sid offered to give Terri and me a ride home, which I felt comfortable with because he hadn't tried to hit on me, and he seemed charming enough to garner Barry's acceptance, which meant a lot to me. We all walked, stumbled, and fell down the street, back to the bar where they were both parked. I waved drunkenly toward Derek. He drove off first. Terri and I got into the car, and I began to feel strangely sober. My body wanted more liquor. My mind wanted escape. After Sid dropped Terri off at home, I asked him to drop me at the store. I couldn't imagine going to sleep without another drink. It was morning now; the corner store would be just opening.

He agreed, but when we stopped, it was in a driveway, not at the store. I looked around and asked what was going on. He said he would be right back, that he just needed to pick up some money and that he would take me to the store next. I watched the day grow lighter and began to feel uneasy. The car seemed to be teetering slowly, as though it were on the edge of a cliff. I have no idea how long it really was, but it felt like he had been gone for hours, and I had no choice but to follow his steps toward the apartment building.

I didn't knock; instead, I simply walked in. I looked around the room and found Derek on the couch sleeping.

"Sid?" I yelled out. There were two large clouded cups sitting to my left with ice melting in them. I smelled the cups and guessed that it was rum and cola. I walked deeper into the apartment and found Sid asleep.

103

I tried to shake him, explaining that I needed to go home. He didn't move so I began poking him in the head. He slapped my hand away and told me that he needed to sleep for an hour or two before driving again. He told me to go lay down in the other bedroom.

I tried to explain to him that I didn't feel well. My stomach was screaming, I pleaded, only for him to fall back asleep, snoring loudly. Giving up, I stumbled into the other bedroom and passed out on the bed. I awoke naked, with a hot body pressing against my back, my butt. I was disoriented and unsure if I was home; had someone broken in to the apartment? When I adjusted my eyes, seeing clearly a sparse bedroom and white sheets around me, I became immediately sick, scared, confused. I tried to get up but the body pushed me back down, grabbing my wrists and holding them as it pushed my entire face and body into the soft bed below. I struggled just to turn my head to the side so that I could breathe, but rather than breathing, I tried to scream. The scream was pathetic, lacking in power due to that night's cigarettes and alcohol. I heard a voice say, "Oh, shut up. We did this last night and you wanted it. Don't be a prude now."

The voice was familiar, yet I couldn't place it. My body flopped around like a fish until the voice demanded that I stop moving. It was a serious voice. The night before began to replay in my mind: the drinks, the religious discussion, the after hours, waiting in Sid's car. I felt fingers around my vagina thrusting and searching, unable to find a hole.

"This doesn't seem to be working out," the voice said, amused. "I think we'll have to try something different. I'll make you a deal, if you stop moving around and trying to scream, I won't hit you in the back of the head with my pistol."

The voice placed itself. Now a hard object was being thrust around farther back. I was careful not to scream, but when it penetrated my ass, I felt a pain like none I had ever felt in my life. I tried to push it out, but it pushed back, harder. Sid was behind me, raping me, and I was stuck, a stripper, a lush, being fucked, and all because I wanted more drink. All I could think was that I deserved this, had it coming. I thought I had no choice, so I laid there and took it. My mind wandered to what would happen when he was done. Would I have to find out where I was and walk home? My mind trailed backward now, further, to the dead body.

When Sid removed himself I felt too uneasy to move. He turned me over and called me a freak, saying he wanted to try that for a long time and couldn't find anyone freaky enough. "You're a freaky ass bitch," he said. I couldn't move. He left only to come back into the room later, and this time Derek was with him.

"Go ahead, man, she's still out, you can probably get some," I heard through a thick layer of fuzz that had formed in my mind, clouding reality. I heard Derek refuse angrily and say something about the police and how Sid shouldn't have brought me here. Suddenly, I saw black.

When I awoke again it was Derek, shaking me roughly. He said that I would probably need to drink in order to combat my hangover. He handed me a small blue cup with plastic flowers punched out on the sides. I thanked him. I took a sip of the liquor, unaware of much, and when I tasted it in my mouth, the fiery consistency seemed to somehow refresh me as a large glass of ice water used to when I was done with a five mile run. Derek said my clothes were in a corner. When I tried to cover up, he reminded me that he had seen me naked at the club many times two nights ago. He helped me up and asked me where I lived. When I told him I didn't remember, I knew that something was wrong.

"You really should stop drinking," he offered, but I wasn't so sure this was just a hangover. Suddenly I became very angry and shot out of the bed and into my clothes with a sudden fit.

"Are you taking me home?"

"Yeah, I suppose," he said.

I didn't want him to know where I lived, so I told him to let me off at Summit Street. I was missing my bag with my shoes, money, and three dancing outfits, so I asked him where it was. "I remember putting it in the back of Sid's car," I said.

He cringed, "Sid left for good this morning. You were like his send-off.," he laughed a little after saying this. "He's being shipped out today to North Carolina."

"What happened to me last night?"

"You mean two nights ago?"

"I was at your house for two days?"

"You got drunk, honey," he laughed meanly. "And just think, if you would have just let me take you out on a normal date, none of this would have happened."

I looked down as though in shameful agreement. He reached over me and opened the door, giving me a slight push to get me out.

"You know, Sid is a Christian," he said. "He was just teaching you a lesson."

A small, muscular man with a bald head was outside of the car now and helped me to my feet. He said that he knew where my bag was and he would show me to it. I plopped in front of the television and waited as though I were a mere guest. When was I going home? Where was I? The man sitting on the edge of the couch tipped a bottle toward me. I took it, allowing myself to fall backwards into fantasy.

I blacked out, and much of this story ends here for me now, but it is quite possible that it goes on further.

Easter

I walked in my front door and greeted the walls that kept me warm, the refrigerator that harbored beer but not much else, and finally the television. I turned it on, watched cartoons through the bad reception, and I finished my drink. It took a while before I realized that my bag was gone and with it all my money, my ID, my outfits. I had lost all my money again. I knew I wouldn't see those guys again. Honestly, I didn't want to.

After a few hours, I noticed a tingle in my leg, spreading quickly. I focused on the TV, beginning to feel lost in the fuzzy-filtered screen; I wondered how long it had been since I called Dad. Where was Barry, and why had he left me? A commercial came on that displayed a set of pastel markers. I began to try to shake my leg awake, but the numbness remained. I realized I was shaking and I pulled a pillow over my chest, hugging it, focusing on the commercial. I grew afraid as I watched the kids on screen draw shapes on hardboiled eggs. I watched them hide their eggs one by one, skip around with baskets. Easter was approaching. I tried to drink some water, but the liquid wouldn't go down my throat, and I choked it back up. Something was wrong.

My body held me captive until I was detoxified. I won't get into details because I dislike reading about such things, but I'll sum it up: I got sick, mentally and physically, and stayed sick. I trembled and braced myself as each cell in my body worked to push out all the toxins that I had spent so much time consuming over the last few weeks; the process took about a week. Then, another Easter arrived.

I was seven years old when Dad told me that I was using my time inefficiently. He said my sister and I should become productive and banished us from the front room where our treasured Saturday morning cartoon and sitcom characters lived. "Life is not about watching, it's about living," he said. The withdrawal was immediate, painful.

After a few respectable hours of "production" — mostly in the form of coloring — I came to realize that nothing could atone for the absence of television. I searched through my toys, dusting them off and then tossing them aside until I found my Sweet Secrets doll. She wore her hair in blonde pigtails and had a round body with a large pink gemstone stuck in her belly. Her head and appendages folded into this body, thereby transforming her into a gaudy piece of plastic jewelry. I strapped her on my wrist and began wearing her as a bracelet everywhere I went, but it didn't take long before I realized that the doll portion of my bracelet was pathetic substitution for *Designing Women* reruns. "I'm bored with my toys," I complained.

"Deal," Dad said.

I tucked the little blonde head in its pink plastic shell for good, drew a hash mark on the band with one of his expensive art pens, and spoke into it as though it were a microphone, eyes locked on my father as I began. "These new rules are dumb, over." Dad left the room, satisfied. I spoke to the hash mark religiously for a few days. Strangely, the narration made mundane activities, such as pouring juice or feeding our cat, meaningful. It was as though I were the star of my own TV show. I even announced commercial breaks, when there was nothing much going on. Dad was pleased. Mom found my behavior disturbing. They argued about it and I said the whole thing could be remedied by TV.

"I will be looking for my basket of candy in the morning," I reported happily. Mom disliked my newfound creativity. She asked who I was talking to with an accusatory tone. "No one," I said.

This one Easter was the only day we went to a church service as a family. Laura hated it because she had to wear a dress. I just wanted to get the thing over with, get to the Easter basket hunt. Mom seemed tired, but uncharacteristically fixed on the idea.

The service began quietly. The reverend asked something to the effect of "Who loves Jesus?" and the meek crowd surrounding me began to holler as though whoever yelled loudest loved him best. I enjoyed this part and began yelling, too.

I noticed was Dad shifting in the pew, seeming uncomfortable. The service went on. I swung my feet back and forth, watching my lavender dress rise and fall, and began digging through Mom's purse to pass the time between yells and shouts. I enjoyed seeing so many people holler excitedly without shame or regret. It was after the sermon, however, that things went to hell, so to speak.

The kids were filtered toward the church basement, made to sit in a circle on the hard, cold floor, and listen to Big Pam lecture about how to stay out of Hell by "brushing your teeth and listening to your mommas." She said that Hell was everything bad we could think of, mixed together. The concept made me uneasy. Laura, on the other hand, would giggle at the word, and was eventually sent to the church kitchen to sit and think about how unfunny hell was. I was jealous. I knew for a fact that there were graham crackers in the kitchen cupboard. I could make out Laura's dirty blond hair and tiny frame moving around the yellow picnic table that sat in the middle of the room.

In a desperate attempt to join her, I began to laugh, too. "No, no, no. You're too old to think that's funny. I'm on to you, Red," Big Pam scolded. "Go sit in the corner and think about what Hell means to you."

"My name is—" I began.

"Shhh," she said. "Listen to Gawd." And she pointed toward the sky. I looked up; a pock-marked ceiling told me all I needed to know. "Listen to what he tells you. Over there. In the corner." Now she pointed to her right and I trudged in its direction.

After plopping down in the corner, I pulled my Sweet Secret bracelet out of my little pink and white purse and lifted the hash mark to my lips. I had a lot of reporting to do. I told the band that Hell meant being back in that circle of horrified children, listening to Big Pam holler, watching her chin skin jiggle each time she threw the word *Gawd* at us like he were a stone.

Later that day, when we told Mom that we had a horrible time and never wanted to go back, she shrugged. "Okay." *Praise Gawd,* I thought, but for some reason I began to worry about Hell. Part of this worry may have stemmed from the fact that I couldn't find my Easter basket. My sister and I searched for hours with only vague hints from Dad, and eventually we gave up, exhausted.

"Today is Monday. Yesterday was Easter and I still haven't found my basket, over," I reported to my wrist band after breakfast.

"Where are you, sweetie? Are you talking to yourself again?" Mom's voice held a delicate mixture of worry and amusement.

You won't let me watch television, so what else am I supposed to do? I thought. I said. "No. I'm just looking for my basket." I pushed out my bottom lip for sympathy as she entered the living room and it worked. Immediately Mom called to Dad, demanding that he give me a better clue.

"Okay, okay," he conceded, "You're warm, warmer…colder… warmer," he continued with this until I was "hot." When he said I was "on fire" near the fireplace I wondered if it was a sick joke. Was this really supposed to make up for the Smurfs?

"Okay, now I'm at the fireplace and I'm hot. But I don't see my basket anywhere." I crouched down. "I'm going in, over." My hand reached up the chimney, feeling around until…"I've got it!"

The basket was large that year and when my Dad stuck it up the fireplace he probably didn't think that it would take twenty minutes of prodding with an old wooden broom or that a clutter of cinder and debris would tumble down with it as it fell. All the candy was wrapped and safe.

"Next year, you'll be looking until your birthday kiddo," he chuckled. Mom rolled her neck back in mock-exhaustion before showing a faint smile, and fainter approval. "Go help your sister now,"

"Okay," I mumbled, bouncing up the stairs with a dark chocolate bunny head in my mouth. Laura cried all day Easter in an underhanded attempt to get Dad to give in. It didn't work. Mom yelled at him. In the morning Dad told Laura her basket was in her room and we hadn't seen her since. When I arrived she was huddled over a large chocolate bunny of her own. Laura's tongue pushed at the bunny's eye socket in a determined way and I told her to bite the whole head off. We laughed about our decapitated bunnies and spent the next twenty minutes testing our stomachs' capacity for candy.

When my Sweet Secrets strap broke later that day I went to my parents, expecting them to send me to the corner to repent. Instead, they warned me against being so rough on my toys, but because I loved it so much they would buy me another, better strap for my Sweet Secrets doll. I told them not to bother, I was a bad kid, undeserving. They told me to go ahead and watch an hour of television. Thinking about this now, it seemed our family was a sitcom in of itself, full of awkward comedy and false starts.

***

More than a decade later, after detoxifying, my body felt hollow. I suppose it was. I called my mother and she told me she would leave her key in the mailbox if I wanted to stop by and she wasn't home. I cannot say if she knew something was wrong by the tone of my voice, but somehow I think she must have. "Stay the weekend with me," she offered. I said I might.

I walked. The sidewalk sucked at my feet. I had three slowly healing gashes on a huge goose-egg above my eye. I had got in a fight after the night with Derek and Sid; I barely remembered it, only my forehead hitting the corner of a concrete step. Half way, the walking began to get difficult. I had to stop many times and sit. I was dying and could feel the lack of nutrition and extreme instability flowing in my body. I was still pickled with alcohol and chemicals; even the inside of my mouth felt sour and dry. I was about to get really sick, again.

I felt something tearing in my gut that turned and shifted as I took each step. I had to make several stops on the way to Mom's, leaning against posts and porches. One of the porches was occupied by two older women who shooed me off, telling me to go back to the crack house I came from.

"I'm sorry."

One of them pointed. "Get off my porch!"

There were two hookers on 4th and High, standing behind a "Burgers This Way" sign that lit up like an arrow and led to a small diner. They asked me if I needed help and I began to cry. By this time, I felt like I had been walking for hours, but the entire walk was less than a mile. One of the hookers was overweight. I remembered laughing and watching my friends throw rocks at those hookers when I was in sixth grade. I turned back toward my apartment. I couldn't make it.

After reaching my front door again, my stomach pushed at my throat. I got inside the door and left Mom a lengthy apology on her voicemail. Then, I slowly moved toward my bathroom where I lay down and slept for the rest of the day.

The next day, I woke up hungry. A Hot Pocket took a long time to work through, but this jumble of cheese and preservatives worked miracles for my body. Everything that had tasted acidic the last few days, even the tap water, eventually tasted normal again.

My illness probably should have been treated in a hospital. Alcohol poisoning is a dangerous condition in which the organs begin to shut down, starting with the liver, when the tissues are overburdened by ethanol and the body can no longer eliminate it, causing the nervous system to shut down. And, though I never admitted to the label *alcoholic*, I knew that some kind of illness or allergy had upset my relationship with the liquid depressant—I didn't have to give it up, just cut back. A few weeks after Easter, I decided to get back to my original plan, college.

Feeling better, I would occasionally feel a rush of weakness, bordering on numbness, which would cause my body to wilt. I would sit and shake my legs and arms until they felt normal again. In the habit of drinking constantly, I continued to drink constantly during my rehabilitation. I refilled the jelly jars my mother had let me have so often that I found it more reasonable to simply drink out of a pitcher that I kept beside me at all times. Eventually, I could even drink wine again.

I hear that alcoholism is an adaptable disease, more of an allergy than a tendency toward extreme usage. I have since attended a few AA meetings in my lifetime, and I highly recommend this compassionate fellowship to anyone who is abusing alcohol, or, as some would argue, being abused by alcohol. For me, it would take a long time to even watch my consumption yet. At the time, it still fed me. I was still trying to indulge an adult storybook fantasy that had long ago yellowed, curled at the edges and crumbled as I tried to flip the page. Alcohol was just a subtle escape that had lost its luster.

The next few days, I thought about my bout with alcohol poisoning often between sips of my daily wine cooler, which didn't taste as good as it once had. A few weeks after Easter, I decided to get back to my original plan, college.

Mom picked me up for lunch that weekend. Upon seeing my apartment for the first time, she was excited. "You have your own digs. You're an adult now," she said, hugging me. I felt pathetic. *You should've seen it a few days ago.* I tried to rush her tour, made sure to keep a cigarette lit the whole time; there was a subtle sour smell that wouldn't dissipate, even though I had collected everything that surrounded my sickness into a large yard bag and hauled it out back.

"So how've you been, all on your own?" she asked. I hadn't been returning her calls over the past few weeks. Thick bangs covered a welt on my forehead, another memento from my last hoorah.

"It's been a strange adjustment, but I think I'm going to be okay."

I pulled away from Mom's embrace because I didn't want her to see me up close. I showed her around. The freshly washed cement-brick walls and steam-cleaned newness of the place made a new beginning feel possible. Wounds heal.

Second Childhood

A therapist of mine referred to the succeeding years of my life as a "second childhood." She explained that I had cut my first one short by leaving home at age fifteen; therefore, she said, I craved stability as I matured, belatedly. I liked this theory. Developmental psychology breaks life down into easy, compact stages, and blames most of my problems on the interruption of these stages. From the ages of fifteen to eighteen, according to common developmental theory, a teenager is just beginning to acquire a clear sense of identity and morality, which gives me a nice, comfy excuse for perverse behavior.

"Your decision to embark on this second childhood was really the manifestation of a desire to recreate the stability you might have had if you hadn't left home," the therapist explained; I repeated her words often.

1998: In true, childlike fashion, it seemed necessary that I sit around and feel sorry for myself for quite some time before moving on; but this stubborn lull occurred alongside a growing desire—maybe supplying the motivation—to change my lifestyle. I didn't stop drinking, but when I tasted alcohol, it wasn't quite the same. I remember long conversations that I had on paper, writing to my father, my mother, anyone, in which I made apologies, confessions, and resolutions. Much of this time is useless to relive now, and so my brain has filtered it away, sparing daily thoughts from unnecessary interruption.

The path from college enrollment to graduation was obvious to me: it meant drastically altering my surroundings, just one more time, in order to make it work. I had to start over.

Mom's hair was now the color of wet clay, and she seemed to glow at our lunch that day. When I told Mom I had quit dancing, she responded with an extended, uncomfortable silence. I waited her out for a time, and then asked if she heard. I knew she had. Finally, she put her hands palms down on the table and leaned in, searching my face for authenticity, searching, it seemed, for a smile, a hint of deception. Finding no evidence, she said, "Oh, thank God." Then she repeated herself. My mother thanked God more times than I remember, and it was a god that I had no idea she believed in.

I considered my mother's smooth tan face. Her acceptance felt good, addictive even. I wanted more.

"I'm thinking I want to get serious about college," I went on. "I even have a little money stashed, but I don't know how to do it, what to study."

"It doesn't matter, sweetie, you take a bunch of basic courses before you have to decide what you major in." Mom had been a college student at one time. She had planned to teach special needs children, but had dropped out twenty credits before graduation.

I watched Mom poke at her Reuben with a fork and lift the top piece of marbled bread to scrutinize the layers of corned beef below it. The amount of meat on the sandwich was pathetic and I wondered if she'd send it back.

"Look, Mom, I'm sorry."

She looked around for our waitress. Not seeing anyone, she shrugged and took a bite of the sandwich. "Sorry for what, honey?" she asked.

"I'm just sorry for being...."

Mom put down her sandwich and moved to the side of the booth I was sitting in. She put an arm around me and brushed the hair off my face. I pulled back. "Don't apologize to me. I worry about you, but your decisions are yours. You're the one that will have to deal with them," she said.

"You think I can get my shit together?"

"That's up to you," she said stoically and moved back to her seat. She told the sandwich, "You're going to have to be tough. You've got a tough road."

"I'm done with the tough road," I said defensively, definitively. Mom didn't argue. "First, I have to find a good job."

***

Finding the perfect minimum wage job was about as easy as forcing size six thighs into size two capris. I tried a few places and quit soon after. I was used to quick, disposable cash, new clothes, late nights, high heels, and a blurry five-hour shift that ended in deep drunken sleep. My earlier diet of nutritious food and my habit of eight hours of nighttime sleep had ceded ground to sugary coffee and sugary alcohol, sleep optional.

Here, I made my rounds. I started at White Castle part-time and quit two days later. It took another four to get the onion smell out of my clothing. I tried a factory job where I separated uniforms into different lines and tag routes, and quit a month later because I couldn't wake up early enough to get there on time. I tried waitressing but my short-term memory was horrible and I often confused orders or refilled water with Sprite, which one lady explained to me was "a criminal thing to do to a diabetic." I quit that job, too.

Finally, Elisa suggested I work for her, at a prom dress store in the mall. It would be a good temporary job—the store was going out of business—until I found something else. Elisa's boss had quit after the bankruptcy announcement, and she had recently been promoted to manager. The interview process would consist of two questions: would I buy her a drink that night, and would I promise not to come into work slobbering drunk all the time? I said I would promise nothing and she hired me anyway. It was an easy job. There was no order to the store now that it was closing, simply rack after rack of prom dresses, gloves, and gaudy jewelry that we would have to pick up off of the floor and put back on the racks when customers knocked them over. Everything was seventy percent off and those items that had no ticket were either five or ten dollars, depending on whether we liked the customer. Welcome to retail.

I got a part-time at another department store, thanks to my "experience" working at the prom dress shop. I worked in jewelry, and the day I started I met a woman named Candice. She said she was retired and told me that she was just working the job for the discount. I never saw her buy anything, so I suspected she just needed to get out of the house. She was the only fifty-eight year old woman that I had ever met who found sheer delight in fart jokes. And no matter what she was laughing at, her joy was infectious.

Whenever I had a particularly condescending or demanding customer, I would give her the signal. She'd walk over and stop right next to the unsuspecting man or woman. She would then bark, "Are you giving this customer a hard time? Excuse me, are you receiving adequate service? Because this little lady is barely hanging on." She would turn to me and I would cower. "You know you left the Windex out last night? Huh? You know what? You're on notice, just remember that, and after you're finished with this customer we will have a long talk." She would then turn to the customer again and sigh. "These young people today have no respect."

The customer would either stand there, stunned, or defend me. Candice would walk away saying, "Oh, don't pity her. She should know better."

Then, like clockwork, the previously demanding customer would apologize to me on her behalf and proceed to purchase the more expensive watch or bracelet, whichever item I had recommended, which was always the item that would pay me higher commission. One customer felt so bad for me that she handed me a business card, and promised an interview if "that horrible woman" fired me or I wanted to quit. When I worked with Candice, she put most of the sales on my number, so that I made more money. Why she did this for me, I couldn't quite figure.

Candice and I bonded over my current pledge of abstinence, which had not stemmed from religious reasons but an unshakable distrust of men. She found this endearing. She loved telling me horror stories about her ex-boyfriends, her ex-husband, her father—the men who neglected her, abused her. She could laugh at it now, she said, because she had taken control over her life. I felt comfortable enough to confide in her my own horrors, fears.

Candice's disdain for our clientele was extraordinary. I still chuckle when I recall her reaction to the more annoying variety of customer: the rude, impatient, haughty, demanding, argumentative, or parsimonious. When she would encounter these cases, Candice would interrupt the customer by a loud slap to her chest. "Oh!" She would start. The girls who worked across the way, in scarves, would smile knowingly while the poor customer stood there stunned, probably worried that Candice was having a heart attack. She would evaluate the victim before going on. "Oh, my! That tuna salad sandwich is coming up. Oh! Oh! Excuse me for a moment." She would then walk away as I resisted the urge to clap. Other times, she would release an impressive amount of bodily gas, apologize to the customer, and repeat. I would play along, ask her where her medication was, but by this time the customer would have excused himself, having gone to buy the same mediocre *Fine Jewelry* at a different department store.

After I had been working with Candice about a year, she started to ask me odd personal questions. "What are you really working here for?" she asked. "What are you going to do next? Do you have a five-year plan?"

"No," I said. "I don't know. I took a few courses this year. Maybe psychology, but I don't really don't have a plan yet."

"Oh, so you're *undecided*, I see."

When Candice said the word, I heard criticism and it hit me with a whack. She sounded judgmental, and her judgments were for others, customers, not me. Meanwhile, I knew she was right. I had been undecided since I started school. I had spent all the money I had from dancing, and had even racked up almost two thousand dollars in debt from a nasty shopping habit I had picked up at the mall. I had no boyfriend, few friends, and a lingering drinking problem; rather, a lingering inclination to stay drunk. I could barely pay my bills. My apartment was the size of a large bus stop. I was pushing my rock up the hill again and, again, going nowhere. Lucky for me, Candice had a solution.

"I never knew what I wanted to do at your age, either. Hell, I didn't know that until last year when I decided to open a beauty salon. And guess what? I'm finally doing it. I'm opening my very own salon sometime in February."

"Wow, congratulations," I started and she put her hand up.

"Thank you, thank you," she said, standing, curtseying, "but listen, there's more. I have a proposition for you."

We were sitting at lunch together next to the food court. Plastic trees swayed in the air-conditioning. A man behind me was pedaling samples of Bourbon Chicken on tiny toothpicks. I watched Candice's mouth move as she summarized her plan. "Well, you remember how you thought it was really cool to work in a salon, and how proud you were of me for opening one?"

"Yeah." I thought she might offer me a free haircut, and I got excited.

"Well, I was thinking about offering you a job. You could work for me as a receptionist and maybe even go to beauty school. I looked into it. If you want to be a manicurist, it's only about three months of school."

"I'd love to work for you. Thanks, but, um, it's not realistic." I listed my concerns: I had no car and the bus system in Columbus was derisory; I had no money for schooling, for supplies, for a move.

"I thought of all that. Here's the second part of my proposition. You can live with me and Ted in Washington Square. We could drive you to the salon and you could take the bus to school."

I had never been to Washington Square, but it had a reputation as the wealthiest part of town. People referred to it as an island of old money, tucked between the near east side of downtown Columbus and a sprawling ghetto. I snapped out of the moment, and attempted to picture myself there, in a mansion-like home on a hill, looking down toward the slums, where I belonged. I couldn't take her up on this offer. It wasn't realistic.

"It would be too much of an inconvenience," I insisted.

"None at all." She clapped her hands. "Listen, I only offer this to you because I have a lot of faith in you. You wouldn't owe me a thing, and you'd be helping me out, too. So what do you think?"

"Candice, are you seriously offering to put me through school and let me live with you?"

"Slow it down, I said you could live with me while you go through school, but you'll have to pay for it yourself. I don't just have a few thousand dollars lying around. A lot of our money is invested in this business, and it's taken a long time to get off the ground. I'm so anxious about the whole thing. Part of the reason I've been working this little job is to keep myself distracted while I wait."

"A few thousand?" This seemed impossible. "What about rent?"

"I'll waive rent. And I'll let you work for us as a receptionist while you're in school. Pay you ten dollars an hour, so that you can make payments on your school. It will be fine if you're willing to go through with it."

My parents thought it was a scam. Mom asked me if I was sure I really knew this woman. I said that I did; Candice was my friend. I had honestly thought a lot about turning down her offer solely because of Ted, the boyfriend, and the fact that I hadn't met him. He might not be supportive of Candice's whimsical idea; he might be a pervert; I might annoy him. What if I recognized him? What if he had been a regular at the club, they guy who always got private dances and asked for extra?

Candice was persistent.

"I'm still not sure," I told her a few days later.

"It's up to you, but think about it rationally, Jen. Windfalls don't come every day, and do you know I would have killed for an opportunity like this when I was your age? That's why I'm offering. Just make sure you really think about things. Maybe we could pay some of your tuition even. I think we can deduct that as a business expense. Let me look into it."

As I heated up a Hot Pocket, I looked around at the cement walls and stand-up shower that I was renting. The furniture was musty and covered with thick blankets, because most of it had been sitting in front of the dumpster when I moved in. Most everything I owned that was worth anything consisted of clothing, making the task of moving simple. My life was condensed into a few boxes, a lamp, a stained-glass panel that my father had made, and a few trash bags full of clothes.

Candice was a night owl, so I called her around eleven. She answered the phone promptly and said she was watching a new show called *Sex and the City*, and she told me I should have been there to see Ted's face when the sex scenes were on. She was laughing. Her life seemed like so much fun. "I'm moving in," I said.

"There you go."

After I hung up the phone, I began packing. No cost could outweigh the benefit of leaving. I woke Candice up the next morning to work out the details. Hours later, she stood in my apartment with coiffed blonde hair and dressed in chinos and a form-fitting white top that accentuated her tanned skin. She looked around at my living space as though it were an accident scene.

"Is that supposed to be a kitchen?"

"The entire place is a shit hole," I said.

"You deserve better. And you'll get it." She punched me in the arm and began to laugh. "We're going to put you on track. You're *my* family now."

Candice told stories about her boyfriend and the stuffy people that surrounded him as we hauled my stuff out to her car. Her tales were hilarious full of nosey neighbors, white picket fences, and luxury cars. She said she didn't fit in, and that she was lonely in her lifestyle. I would be an ally.

Washington Square World

When I announced that I would be moving in with my co-worker, the general response was confusion. "Who are these people?" Laura asked over the phone, our first conversation in months.

"Why would they take you in like this?" Dad wondered after I told him what my new address was. I had expected trepidation from my family, but the strongest reaction came from Elisa. After I broke the news she looked sickened, possibly worried.

"Washington Square? If you look at someone the wrong way there it makes the news for weeks. Weeks, girl. Everything that happens to people with that much money is either glamorous or tragic. It's not real life. It's a fucking soap opera."

"The attention sounds nice," I said. "If I die, I'd rather make the news than be just another rumor around the neighborhood."

"I'm confused. Why are these people doing this?"

"It's an opportunity, Elisa. I'm friends with this lady. I know it sounds strange, but I'm ready to do something, anything different." She was quiet. She explained that she was too busy to celebrate with me. The next day, she didn't answer her phone.

I wondered what I had done. Was it my drinking? Was it her new boyfriend, whom I knew didn't like me? Whatever it was, I didn't want to accept it. I called, left notes in her mailbox, apologizing for whatever I had done. No little thing like moving to a nice neighborhood could alienate her, right? After all, *her* family was well-off.

The day I moved was bittersweet. I really wanted to call Elisa, but I still couldn't reach her. There was no one else to call.

My blood pressure dropped and a weakness spread through my body as I entered the room that was to be mine. I felt a mixture of excitement and intimidation, but mostly I was just scared. "This used to be the maid's quarters when I was growing up," Ted said. He was a tall man with thick, dark eyebrows. He was definitely not a regular at any strip club.

"You have no idea what this means to me, sir," I said.

"You're welcome." With an anxious smile, Ted began reflecting upon his childhood in a deep resounding voice that echoed through my head as I surveyed the room. "This house has been in my family for generations. Actually, many of the homes on this street have second and third generation owners. That's rare in our states."

I nodded, taking in the private bathroom with a silent sigh. I pushed up on the window next to the bed and it caught at about a half an inch. Maybe they didn't want the maid to escape I thought, but kept the joke to myself. From the window I could look down at a spacious backyard. Two small white dogs stopped what they were doing, acknowledging me from below.   One stared at me, punctuating its surveillance with threatening yips, while the other barked steadily at the fence next to him. I looked over at the fence expecting a neighbor dog or cat, some sort of provocation, and couldn't pinpoint a thing.

"Ted, stop boring her with your stories. She doesn't want to hear that, do you?" Candice asked me.

I shrugged and asked whether the dogs were allowed up here in my room. "They look like they want to eat me. Or, at least one of them does. That other one is picking a fight with the fence."

Candice clapped her hands. "Oh! I have to introduce you to my babies!"

"What are their names?"

"Biff and Benny."

"I think Benny's confused," I said pointing at the dog, which was now waving a paw in the air, still facing no one.

"Oh no, that's Biff. He's blind." I watched Biff yap at the fence and wondered just how long I would be able to stay at the house. The plan was contingent on how long it would take me to get through cosmetology school, and then Candice said I should save up enough for a down payment on a nicer apartment. It would probably take a few months.

Ted began to tell me about the veterinarian's training and how she was the best in town, and why. "Biff was born blind because his head was too big for a normal birth and on the way out his eyes were damaged."

"Really?"

"Oh, anyways," Candice interrupted again. "The pretty girl here doesn't want to hear about that." Ted's indifference to her interruptions confused me, and made for some awkwardness. I glanced around again, set my final bag on the bed and patted the mattress for firmness, not really noticing whether it was comfortable or not. Nerves did this to me then, masked ordinary sensory comforts.

They let me get settled, and I was relieved to be alone. My "quarters" were larger than any apartment I ever lived in. It was the third floor of a home in one of the richest parts of Columbus. The neighborhood was full of old money overflowing with rigid expectations for the people who lived there, Candice said, a sort of warning. I would find out exactly what she meant.

I smoked Newport 100s now and felt that my cigarette breaks had become twelve minute meditations instead of eight. I needed cigarettes, or maybe the alone time that went with them. Yet, as deep as my love affair with smoking went, I stood awkwardly with my cigarettes in front of the house. I felt as though the air was cleaner here. My lengthy cigarette was dirty, and evoked a strange sort of displacement, visible proof I didn't belong.

Two days into my new residency and four minutes into my cigarette, a police cruiser pulled into the drive. He asked me what I was doing on the property, and when I explained that I was living with Candice, he seemed skeptical, drawing his head back. "That's funny. I thought Ted lived here." His voice was sharp.

"Ted." I repeated. "Yes. Ted lives here—I mean, I'm living with him and Candice."

"Oh! Is that Ted's aunt, the one that's been staying here?"

I laughed. Candice told me this happened a lot and that I should smack anyone who misunderstood. "No. Candice is Ted's girlfriend, or, uh, common-law, or something like that."

"The woman who has been staying here in Ted's house is his girlfriend?" He hung half way out of the police car now, but remained seated. His moustache was a straw-like patch of hair over his mouth; moustaches always made me suspicious if unaccompanied by a beard.

"Do you want to speak with her? Or Ted?" I asked, hoping he would leave. "I can get them."

"I suppose that won't be necessary," he said and turned away. I thought I heard him repeat the word girlfriend under his gossipy breath. "Take it easy," he said and pulled out of the driveway. I lit another cigarette. This one tasted good, full. I waited for the cruiser to disappear, and then stuck my middle finger in the air, directing it at each house within view on the street, hoping that whoever called the police got the message.

***

Candice had an acute capacity for noticing detail. When I came home after a weekend at my father's house she would tell me, before any scale could, that the extra pound or two I was carrying looked good on my face, but not on my ass. "You better watch," she would say. "You have an athletic build but that's the type that gets big fast."

She would notice other things, too. Like when I was almost out of shampoo (despite my having a private bathroom) and when I used an extra half-scoop to make the morning coffee. "Wow, I can tell who made the coffee this morning!"

Ted would take a sip, look intently at the corner of the room, and shrug, "How so?"

It wasn't just me, either. Candice would notice when the CVS clerk dyed her hair and when the lady who always smoked in front of Kroger's was wearing a new pair of gold-rimmed glasses. She also had a genuine interest in all these details, which I can only imagine would become tiresome.

I had felt cozy in her home at first, but uneasiness began to set in. I sat at the solid walnut table in the kitchen, blinking my eyes furiously. Something in the house made my allergies flair. I was drinking my fourth cup of Ted's watery coffee. He was bombarding me with trivia.

"Did you know that Columbus was almost called Ohio City?" he asked.

"Really? Why'd they change it?"

"Yes, really. The Ohio General Assembly selected the name Columbus due to one gentleman's fascination with Christopher Columbus. I guess he fancied the explorer as a hero."

"Huh." I watched the door for Candice. I felt unable to sustain the conversation or to absorb his trivia. I was in dire need of someone else to take the stage. Candice, with her wit and fart jokes, her trivial gossipy stories, allowed me to rest. I heard the car pull in the drive and cast my eyes toward the ceiling in relief. "I think Candice's home."

Ted and the dogs raced to the front door. The dogs jumped up and down at the door. "Hi, sweetie," he said. I hurried to lay out all the silverware for the surprise dinner Ted and I had prepared for Candice and her daughter, Lindsay, whom I'd met before but never really talked to at length.

"What's all this?"

I turned to see her small, round frame in the doorway. "It's for you," I said.

"Well, look, at, this! You mean I don't have to cook? Hell, I don't know if I can handle this."

"Handle it," I said and pulled out a chair for her.

"Wow, did Ted help?"

"Yeah, he took care of the vegetables. And I learned a lot about, well, everything."

"You poor thing," she said. "Have you been boring her, Ted?" she teased. "You two! I really appreciate this. My redheaded stepchild." I'd heard this before. She patted my head and then took a seat.

Ted sat, too. He said Lindsay was out in the car, refusing to come in. She was mad at Candice. I couldn't tell why.

"Oh, let her have her little tantrum."

Lindsay was thirty-something. She had a seven year old son named Bradley. She called her mother every half hour, and, if she did not, Candice called her. Their conversations were unproductive, going something like this:

"Hey,"

"Hey."

"What are you doing'?"

"Nothing. Just sitting here."

"Oh, did you tan?"

"Yeah."

"Anything else going on?"

"No."

"Okay, bye."

"Call me later."

These conversations were vital to Candice. She craved them. And if Lindsay's phone was busy, or she didn't answer, Candice would pace and dial and dial until she got through.

I would find out later that just prior to my invitation to 42 Washington Square, Lindsay had lived there with her son. It was only when she threatened to take Bradley and move in with her ex-boyfriend that Candice shook enough money out of Ted to buy her daughter a house a block and a half away. "This was necessary," Candice explained to me, "because Lindsay is handicapped. She can't drive."

She wore thick glasses, but I couldn't figure an obvious handicap. "What's wrong with her?"

"She's blind."

Later, I would become suspicious of Lindsay's handicapped status. I would recall all the times I answered the door to find Lindsay there with Bradley in hand, keen to observe a new item of clothing I had on; she even noticed more subtle shifts in my appearance. "Hi," she would say, "I like your hair. Is that a new headband?" So I asked Ted about it later. He said that she was blind in one eye and her vision was inadequate for nighttime driving, but other than that she was fine. He looked around before adding, "And I think she should get a job."

This tension between Ted's idea of parenting and the way Candice treated Lindsay was made evident after dinner one night. Candice and Ted sat in their armchairs, Lindsay on the couch and me on the floor against the couch. We were all just finishing up the meal and talking about the shop. "I think we should put tanning beds in the salon," Candice said to Ted. "At least two of them."

"I don't know."

"Yeah, tanning beds would be real good, Mom," Lindsay said.

"I don't know that we have the clientele," I observed, thinking about the number of roller sets our shops did on gray heads. The number of clients under fifty was miniscule.

"She has a point," Ted said through a mouthful of ice cream. "You should tan," Candice said to me, lifting her eyebrows. "You may feel different after you tan."

Lindsay jumped up. "Yes, come on I'll show you how." She grabbed at my arm, which I pulled back gently.

"No, no, I don't tan. I burn. I have red hair, freckles, you know, like the girls in the sunscreen commercials. In the skin cancer awareness posters. I don't think it would work."

"But you don't have a lot of freckles, so you should be fine."

I looked at Lindsay. I had never visited her house, but I knew it had a tanning bed like her mom's. Her skin was the color of a chestnut—a very authentic looking tan, except for a few small patches of white that surrounded her eyes. There were also white rings around her neck where it naturally creased. "You'd look really good," she coaxed.

"Maybe later," I said, and five minutes later I was lying in a neon blue coffin that vibrated slightly. I watched the lights for a moment and then closed my eyes, setting the goggles aside. I thought this must be what it was like to die in a microwave.

The next day my skin was so burnt that it was already peeling.

"See, I burned!" I said, running downstairs.

"Wow, I didn't know people could burn from tanning beds." Candice shrugged. "Oh, well, it's not for everyone."

"Yeah, it's for people that could just go out in the sun and do it the natural way. No one in my old neighborhood would ever tan."

"That's because you were the only white person in your neighborhood."

"Okay, but it's also because poor people have to be logical with their money."

"Oh, so that's why most of them smoke crack?"

My throat filled with air and I gulped it down. The phone rang. Ted said it was for me and handed me the phone. "Hello," I said slowly. The voice sounded distant, as though the person on the other end was calling from the real world. "Dad? Is that you?"

He told me that he had an epiphany. "I'm going to go all the way," he said. He decided to go to graduate school for art, and he was planning to leave town. This was a big decision and he needed me to know about his plans, he said. I told him to go for it. I told him all about my experiences as Candice and Ted's. I praised my hosts and their house, their stuff, and halfway through the conversation I heard a phone click. "Was someone listening?" Dad asked. Someone hung up the phone.

Looking back, this was my first clue that my time at Washington Square might come at some odd cost. My second clue came a few weeks later when I went on a date with a skinny man named Tony, whom I had met at the salon.

Tony was kind and funny, even attractive; tall and slender with a strong, square jaw line. He had moments of dry humor that I enjoyed, but somehow I couldn't allow his conversation to penetrate my wandering mind. It was on my first date since moving into Candice's home, and I wasn't ready for it. I had somehow lost my ability to engage in small talk, and I realized maybe this was a skill I had never fully developed. Thankfully, Tony was content to carry the conversation alone. I learned a bit about OSU basketball, the new sound system installed in his Suburban, and what restaurants served the greatest variety of imported beer. I often smiled throughout dinner and contributed a few words.

As we drove home, just when I began to physically cringe from the monotony of what I was coming to realize a normal date consisted of, everything changed. "Isn't that your Mom?" Tony asked, pointing me toward the rearview. I turned around and sure enough, two cars back, Candice was there peeking at us from just above a steering wheel.

"That's strange."

"She's spying on us. Watch," Tony said, turning right, and then left. Candice turned after us. He laughed. "Should we should park in a dark alley and pretend to make out, just to mess with her?" This playfulness made Tony endearing, but I was too exhausted by his monologue to engage.

"That isn't my Mom," I said. "She's my boss. Maybe we should reschedule the rest of this date," I suggested.

"Okay." He shrugged and drove me back to Washington Square. When we pulled in the drive, he leaned in to kiss me. I turned my head. When I got in the house, I ran directly upstairs, to my quarters.

***

My mother had been suspicious of Candice's motives, and somehow I knew she'd have some insight into this odd episode. I called her, knowing she'd be asleep. Her voice was groggy, but when I said, "Mom, things are getting strange," she seemed to perk right up.

"Aren't they always, sweetie?" She laughed. When I didn't join in, she stopped and asked what was wrong.

"I think Candice is spying on me. I saw her following me when I went out on a date today, and I think she's been listening in on my phone conversations."

"You went out on a date?" She sounded surprised, wounded.

"It was a real date, yeah. I won't see him again, but I got a nice steak dinner."

"Way to go. So that crazy bitch is following you around now, huh?"

"Damn, Mom, I'm not mad, just confused by it all."

"I am. I'm jealous. It feels like I've been replaced, sometimes, so I may be partial—but personally, I think the woman is a nut."

"Never. You'll never be replaced, Mom. Honestly, I'm thinking about moving out soon after I get my license. Would you come over here this weekend? If you can pick me up, I'll buy you lunch. I can show you my 'quarters.'"

***

I sat at the front desk, checking the appointment calendar for the week, highlighting the appointments that had been filled that day. I had three manicures scheduled for next Friday, when I would have my license. In the meantime, I had been working for Candice and Ted as a receptionist, attending Ohio State School of Cosmetology in the evenings. Soon, I would be a licensed nail technician.

Nail school was hardly as riveting as Candice had projected, but I was glad to be there, glad to be out of the club. I took classes for three months, two of them were open book, and the last month was application. Along with a dozen other women, I studied the parts of the human nail, its composition, and the lengthy list of diseases and disorders that it is prone to acquire.

I would usually ride the bus to school as Candice and Ted closed up the shop. It carried me on the east side of town an hour before I had to be there. I would get off the bus at a corner at the end of the shopping center that harbored the school, and after walking around a bit I found a good place to hang out before class: a biker bar named Jim's, or maybe Joe's, Bob's....

Sitting at a bar with a three-letter name, by myself, in the afternoon, five days a week was nothing to be embarrassed about, nothing new or different to me. This is what bar regulars do. But, somehow, as I sat at the corner seat at this bar, studying the difference between Onychatrophia and Onychophagy, I seemed to notice quite a few sideways glances. After a few days of studying, I figured my lack of rapport might have had something to do with my jukebox selections. I tended to cue a Bob Marley song, which would generate audible sighs from the other two regulars. One day, a female bartender actually asked me for my ID. Seeing as how I was twenty, I offered it up. I was shocked when she asked me to leave. The next day, I went back to find a different bartender, and I was grateful enough to steer clear of the jukebox.

A little tipsy, I would arrive at nail school restless and giggly. I marveled at my teacher's mullet and passed notes in class, one of which, I recall, said something about her camel toe. I laughed so hard at the note, which was, by the way, illustrated, that I had to actually run out of the room in order to make it to the bathroom in time.

I doubt I would have received my license had I not had a clear view of another girl's forearm, which was covered in definitions that I would often confuse. When we got our certificates, I thanked this girl, and bought her a drink at the biker bar.

That last day, we sat and laughed about our teacher and some of the other students. We compared the acrylic nail sets we had affixed to the prosthetic hands we each had to purchase for our final, practical exam. The hands looked like they belonged to an extremely tall woman with jaundice. Mine had orange nails, to offset the yellow tone of her prosthetic skin. Her hand had a scarlet and grey French manicure set, with a little block 0 on each thumb. "Mine looks like hell," I said, placing it on the bar by our drinks. We toasted to graduation and exchanged phone numbers, which neither of us would use. After a few drinks, I felt a mean headache coming on and excused myself.

There, at the bus stop, I daydreamed, a recurring habit, only this time I had a backpack, a prosthetic hand, and a case full of small instruments and polishes, my trade tools, beside me. I took deep breaths, to combat my aching head, but all I could seem to smell were chemicals. At graduation, my teachers at Ohio State School of Cosmetology had promised that if we worked hard and established a good clientele, we could make lots of money; we would also have the freedom to set our own hours. I knew I'd love my new career. And I knew the practical application would be far more riveting than the classrooms had been.

***

A few months later, my daydreams had floated elsewhere. I was lucky to get scheduled one manicure (gross income: ten dollars plus a tip) in a day. By the end of one week, I usually did one set of acrylic nails (twenty-five, plus tip), and a few pedicures (twenty, plus tip). When I would arrive in the morning, I'd make the coffee and brood until my first customer arrived. After that first customer, I would have a headache and an attitude. I would sit silently as Candice gossiped about the other employees, people I liked. These co-workers, in turn, told me what Candice had revealed to them about my life: everything I ever told her, only exaggerated.

One day, the salon hadn't yet opened, and already I wanted to leave. Candice was flipping through the magazines in the waiting area. She found an article on AIDS and decided to share it with me. After, she began to tell me what she thought about those afflicted. I ignored most of what she said, then I grew too uneasy to ignore her. "People get this disease because they're not doing what they're supposed to. Promiscuous women and the gays. I love gay people, but there's a reason they get this disease. You see, the bacteria in their butt holes is not meant to touch the penis, so when it does, it spontaneously creates the AIDS virus," she was saying.

What? Was she serious? Normally, when Candice said something extreme it was funny, I'd smile. "Bigot," I muttered. "Bullshit," I said loudly.

"No, it's true." I looked at her in a state of disbelief. "Tell her, Ted."

I looked at Ted. I had so much to say that I wanted to scream. All my thoughts were thrusting and pushing at once, getting caught. To my surprise, Ted—a rational, scientific man—shrugged and said he didn't know what we were talking about. What he was really saying was that he didn't want to talk about it. How could he let her say this?

She went on. "I know this because a doctor friend of mine explained it to me. It is precisely why some women cannot have children, who were too promiscuous when they were younger. They wear their stuff out down there and then it becomes no good. Now, you know I'm not particularly religious, but the facts prove that if we misuse what God gave us, it backfires on us."

"How can you say that? Pain comes into everyone's life sometimes, it's not punishment. No one deserves something like AIDS."

"AIDS is extra painful for a reason."

Candice knew I danced. Was she telling me that I deserved AIDS? "What about cancer? Do people 'deserve' cancer?"

"No. They don't deserve AIDS, either, but it's the result of a bad decision."

"I can't listen to this," I said. I walked outside and paced in front of the salon door. I smoked a cigarette, wondering what exactly made a person think like this. AIDS would just be a start for me, if it were doled out for bad decisions. I thought of Mom's friend Gregory, a man who I had met at an AA meeting with Mom long ago, a gentle man who called me "beautiful" when I was a child; he had recently died of AIDS and I wanted to defend him. As I paced, my muscles began to stiffen, readying for escape. It was time.

At the end of the work day, one of the salon employees who'd come on for the afternoon shift explained to me that Candice had been extremely worried about my "promiscuous" behavior lately. He also told me that Candice had told everyone that I was sneaking liquor into her house.

I had, in fact, snuck a bottle of Paul Mason brandy into her home, but I only ever kept it wrapped up in my pajamas, deep in a large bag that I kept zipped. Moreover, I hadn't had sex with anyone since I lived with her, so I was unsure where she was getting her information. I did worry, however, about the bottle. I never drank from it; it was there for comfort, for necessity. So how did she know? Was she going through my things? Suddenly, I felt restless. That day, I opened the bottle for the first sip of many and my muscles relaxed. I had to go, again, anywhere, to begin again.

PART THREE

THE EDUCATION

Chemistry

Tension continued to build in Washington Square. At the salon, I was often sluggish and sick. I would sit in the backroom and chat with the stylists about how I hated gossip and pedicures. Instead of keeping the coffee area stocked and greeting clientele as I was supposed to, I let the stylists experiment on my hair while I complained to them about how I hadn't been feeling well. When I overheard Candice grumbling to Ted of my laziness, I wasn't surprised.

"I'm sorry if I've seemed lazy," I said, later that evening. Candice didn't look up from the television. "It's these headaches I've been getting, they're worse. They make me nauseous."

"Nauseated," Ted whispered. He was sitting in his recliner at the back of the room, reading a thick hardcover. He didn't look up.

I had been getting brutal headaches since beginning the practical application courses in manicuring, and initially I figured they were stress-induced. Working full-time, I noticed the pain became more consistent and intense. I explained all of this to Candice and Ted during a commercial break.

"It's probably psychosomatic," Candice said. "Your body will adapt to the chemical smell and your headaches will disappear. Look, Jen, there's a new *Sex and the City*." She pointed to the screen. "I think Miranda gets some action in this episode. Come watch, sit by me." She patted the couch.

Acetone, a potent ingredient in nail polish remover, combined with the monomer and polymer mixture I used for acrylic nails, intermingled with fumes from hair dye and perms, hovering in the air at Candice's under-aerated salon each day. As I watched TV, I wondered how I never considered the correlation. I sat on the floor and placed Biff on my lap, trying to calculate the number of chemicals I inhaled each day. His fluffy white body curled as I pet him. Whenever I paused, he rolled over and nudged up at the air beside me.

As Candice made a comment about Sarah Jessica Parker's nose, and I began to wonder if my credits were still good at the community college. I resolved to call the next day, to see what I needed to do to enroll full-time. Psychosomatic or no, between the fumes at work and the tension at home, there was no reprieve. My headaches turned to migraines, and I no longer spent nights with Candice watching TV; instead, I began sneaking bottles into my room, spending time alone, planning my next move.

***

Candice's face was stony when I told her I wanted to move on. She sat across the dinner table, glaring, intimidating me in a maternal, disapproving way. I continued to explain my reasoning. Everything I said came out in jagged, nervous starts. Biff was sitting on my leg as it shook. I petted him anxiously, struggling to speak in full sentences. Ultimately, Candice got up while I spoke. She stopped in the doorway, waited for me to finish. The dog pulled away.

"You're an adult," she said and stomped off. Biff followed her. Ted said he'd go calm her down. He told me not to worry; he said she was just hurt.

"She's so cute when she's mad, isn't she?" he asked. With this comment I began to realize that Ted was mentally ill, just like the rest of us.

My daily headaches vanished but were replaced with uneasiness, guilt. Candice knew I was running away from her. She was familiar with my past because I had told her everything—most everything,—and she thought our relationship was different, special. She seemed to think we were just going through a rough patch in our relationship. Of course, I didn't fully understand why she was so angry, but I felt horrible.

I tried a different approach the next morning. "You know I love you, Candice. I just feel bad, living here for free. I want to make my own way."

"Will you please stop the excuses?" she said with a smile. "We have to get to work. You have some appointments today. Do you think you can survive a few more days?" I didn't answer. She didn't talk to me the rest of the day.

***

When Mom took me to lunch later that week she seemed almost giddy. She had gotten a promotion at work and said she would help me move. "*I'm* your real mother, after all," she said. "You know I'm joking, but in a way I'm jealous of Candice. It seems like she's trying to take my place."

"I never thought of it that way," I said. "But you don't have to worry. She hates me now. I'm not convinced her motives were all about helping me out. It's different than generosity; it's weird, like she wants to *possess* me or something. Does that make any sense?" Mom nodded knowingly. Nothing ever surprised her. We chatted about her new job, her landlord. I asked her if she'd seen Elisa. She said no.

"What happened to her, Jen? You two used to be so close."

I shrugged, explained that I had called my friend weekly since moving to Washington Square.

"Maybe that's not the worst thing," Mom offered. "You two seemed to feed off each other, in a bad way."

After our lunch, Mom took me to Washington Square and we shared a cigarette in the drive. "Candice is probably watching us from the window," I joked. Mom laughed, then checked the window (I did, too) and told me she'd be available when I was ready to start moving my stuff. She offered her apartment—the same one-bedroom loft—and I thanked her genuinely, knowing I couldn't go back.

As I turned my key, I was relieved to hear Candice laughing on the other side of the door. When I said hello she stopped. She stood, lowered her voice and said, "We need to talk." She gestured toward a chair. I sat on the ottoman. "I don't know your mother. And because I don't know her, I'd prefer to be here if she comes to visit, you understand?" I waited for the punch line.

I told Candice that Mom was only sitting in the drive and waiting for me, but she was furious and accused me of lying. I was confused by the severity of her anger. There it was again, redness rising on the skin of the other, the charge of anger blurring reality for both of us.

"What do you have against Mom?"

She looked away, straightening a glass figurine that wasn't crooked. Ted was silent, but his eyes were darting from her to me. "I deserve to know who has been on my property, and who is going to be on my property, right, Ted?" she shot him a glance.

Ted walked over to her and set a large hand on her shoulder. Candice's heart-shaped face was turning redder, and she became very rigid. "Because you're leaving, I expect you to pay me back for the rent I let you slide on, and I expect you to help me find your replacement at the salon. You were an investment." Friendship isn't free.

"So you're not really mad about Mom? You're mad about me leaving? Leaving the salon?"

"No. I'm mad you're ungrateful enough to invite your family, the family who didn't help you before, who let you live in that crap-ass apartment with moldy furniture, who are probably a bunch of white trash, on *my* property without *my* permission." How could I do this to her, she went on. She began to sob as I stood, searching Ted's brown eyes for reason. He wouldn't look at me. I wanted him to say that it was his house, too, that he didn't have a problem with my family. He remained silent.

"I'm moving," I said. "I'll get out of your hair, and you don't have to worry about my 'white trash' family setting foot on your property again. I'll leave. Give me a few days." I was too confused to be angry.

"And you're leaving the salon, too, I assume."

"I can stay at work until you find a replacement," I offered.

"Whatever," she said. She took a long, slow breath and reached two short arms toward me. I would return to real life now; I was relieved. Her arms held me in an uncomfortable embrace, and I prayed it would soon be over. I could smell her anger, a salty irritation offset by the promise of another new beginning to come. Wipe the slate clean, Jen. Relationships like this have to end sometime; I could no longer give her what she wanted.

That empty, uncomfortable embrace did not leave until I did. I moved. I looked for jobs. Ted let me keep the money I had saved on rent while I lived with them; I'm not sure if he told her I had paid him, or whether he actually took a stand for me. He wished me luck. Ultimately, she did, too. I found a job at a restaurant, then at a factory, then a gas station, and I settled into a small apartment with a new friend. Candice found a down-on-her-luck girl who worked at the corner store on Broad Street, and offered her the opportunity of a lifetime.

Driving Lessons

I had been working at the gas station less than a month when my father called me with his "big news."

He said we would have to schedule times we could meet up and he could teach me how to drive his old '84 CRX. "I'm giving you this car. That is, there's a catch. I want you to look after your grandmother, drive her around a little."

"Dad, I can't take care of Grandma. She doesn't like me. Besides, I—"

"She's your family, Jen. Come on, you have to be an adult here." (He was right about that.)

"But—"

"She needs you." He went on to state that this call was to announce the date. He couldn't make me, but he was asking for my help here. "I'm only asking that you take your grandmother to a few appointments each week, shopping on the weekends."

"So this means it's final?"

"It's final. I got into the school in New York, to get my MFA. I'm moving soon and we don't have much time for you to learn how to drive."

"You want to teach me how to drive? And who gets an MFA at forty-five?"

"Yes. And I do. How else are you going to take her to appointments? We need to schedule something soon. I'm giving you an opportunity here, Jen...," he went on.

"Okay, tomorrow morning," I said.

Tomorrow came and so did my father. He looked at my empty apartment with trepidation, almost as though my life might swallow him whole if he stayed too long. I dragged him inside and gave him the grand tour. My roommate, Nancy, shook his hand and hurried out the door. She was a twenty year old who had recently been hired and fired at Candice's salon. We were new friends, both redheads who bonded over our comparable recessive genes and uncomfortable work experiences with Candice. We had begun to go out a lot, to clubs. I liked her innocence and age—she wasn't old enough to drink, so she was always my sober ride home.

Nancy and I owned a bed, a futon, and a chair, along with too much dishware, which her parents had given her, and a kitten that liked to climb legs because there was little else to do. After pulling the claws out of his pant leg, one by one, Dad and I found an empty parking lot a few miles away. The driving lessons began.

"But Dad, I just got a new job. The hours are unpredictable. A car costs money, gas, and I don't have that. I have just enough to make my half of the rent."

"You'll just have to find a better job," he said. "Besides, you get a discount on gas, right?"

Things were this easy. Just get a better job, find a way. I remembered believing things were this easy when I stayed with my mother those last teenaged years. While I stayed up at night, planning, counting dollar signs in the classifieds.

"No," I said.

"You have to learn to drive eventually, right?"

"Not if I move to New York, Washington D.C., um…Boston?"

Dad re-explained that I could not only borrow, but have, this car, and offers like that just didn't come along every day. This pressure wreaked havoc on me; I wreaked havoc on the CRX. Dad was patient as I grinded gears and stalled out repeatedly. We scheduled our next lesson.

***

I waited on the stoop with my stomach in knots as Dad pulled up in the small black car that would soon be mine. It was the same black car that I had heard approaching on Cleveland Avenue the day I asked him to come get me. This day, the car was quiet but its body was far rustier. The tires had all been replaced, but it was still low enough to the ground to get stuck anytime it snowed more than two inches.

"Do you remember when you picked me up that day, when I came back home?" I asked.

"Of course. That was a pretty big day for you," he said. "And for me."

"You pulled up in the CRX. It seemed like more of a junker then."

"Yeah, I put a new engine in it. She runs pretty well now," he said.

My father told me to merge onto the freeway, find out what fifth gear was all about. As I sped up on the on ramp, I was elated, but then a sporty red car rushed past; it seemed like the CRX was shaken by the close call. What followed was a collapse of motor skills. "Fuck!" I immediately jerked my foot.

"Come on, Jen, let up on the clutch gently, and don't be afraid to push on that gas." I listened to my father, but it didn't work. "Push on the gas," he yelled as the car began to buck. I grinded gears, revved gas, and then pulled my foot off the clutch completely, but the car continued to scoot along, traffic rushing all around. I revved again and again before I successfully, consistently, got the thing running at a solid 55 mph, which I would not, no matter what, accelerate beyond.

When we were safely out of death's grip, my father hollered. "Wow, that was scary, Jen, I have to tell you. What's wrong? You were doing better yesterday." He was right. I got the car going and I spent the morning making flawless turns, shifting to neutral when I was breaking, slowly. Dad had been encouraging. "Good job, kiddo," he'd said as I started up flawlessly on a decline.

Perhaps the fact that I had worked myself into a nervous state this day, or that I hadn't slept well, contributed, but I didn't answer him. I was caught up in my thoughts; my calculated movements and rigid shifts were only exasperated by the fact that I was realizing that the reality of this whole scenario was remarkable. It might have happened when I was sixteen had I not left home. What mystified me was the fact that Dad trusted me to take care of Grandma. What reason had I given him to make him believe I would come through? If only he really knew me, I thought.

Safe (relatively speaking) in his bubble of idealism, my father never doubted that I would come around. He had allowed me my mistake and attached a punishment to it: he gave me the independence I sought. When I thought about how much I had concealed from him over the past few years, I felt rather disgusted by myself. I wasn't exactly ashamed of my choices, but I was tired of trying to pretend that everything was always okay. Then again, was it worth it? What would he say if he knew his daughter had been a stripper? That she stumbled around, and passed out in bushes, woke up in strangers' homes. Would he still trust me? I felt like a fraud, but I knew this was my opportunity to truly reconnect with him; it would be a slow process.

That day, my father confessed that I invoked a fear in him like none he said he'd ever felt before. But we had survived, and before I knew it, I was driving. Before I knew it, my father was gone. It was his turn to leave.

***

Grandma was incensed. "Why is your father leaving? What's in New York? Do you think it's that new wife of his that's making him leave town? I swear, that woman has the devil in her. Do you know she yelled at me?"

"Grandma, I'm here to take you to Dr. Bunker's. I don't know how to get there, and I just learned to drive, so we better leave now in case I get lost."

"You, missy...You don't want to drive me around do you? You kids never did appreciate things. You were always spoiled."

My fists clenched. Grandma Gloria had been telling me that my sister and I were spoiled since we were little kids, dressed in thrift store yellow-tag clothing, happy to play with bugs and broken wristbands. I fought the urge to turn around and leave. Then again, this was my opportunity to truly make amends with my father. I was doing this for him. "Grandma, I'm here to take you to Dr. Bunker's. We need to go right now."

She paced her apartment, as though looking for something. "Why did your father just leave me here? Why would he do that? I came here to be close to him, and he leaves me. Everybody leaves me." She grabbed her purse and began to walk toward me. She looked me in the eyes and stopped. "I can't go with you," she said. "I don't trust you. You might leave me there."

On her wall, there was a wooden carving of praying hands, eye level, across from where I stood. The serenity prayer was etched into a plaque beneath the hands. "God, grant me the serenity to accept the things I cannot change," I read. It would become my mantra over the next few weeks.

"What, Jenny? Oh, yes, that's such a lovely prayer, isn't it? Clif gave me that." Clif had been Grandma's boyfriend, until he died of a heart condition. I had only vague memories of meeting him, but I noticed that the thought of him—or perhaps the prayer itself—seemed to drastically alter Grandma's tone. She sat down and began fiddling with one of the buttons on the cuff of her blouse.

"Grandma, please come with me. There's no one else, and I promised Dad I'd get you to your appointment."

"Promised your father," she huffed, forgetting her fond memory (the prayer). "He doesn't care a thing about me."

This day, somehow, some way, we made it to the appointment, only a few minutes late.

Figuring I might increase our odds of arriving to the next appointment on time, I decided to be strategic. I dialed Grandma's number so that she'd be ready to go when I got there. No answer. I drove to her apartment and knocked. I threw small stones at her windows, on the second floor, the way I remembered Dad doing when we were younger. No answer.

I worried that she might be sick or in trouble and unable to answer the door. Her windows were all clouded and I couldn't see inside, other than the subtle hue of her pink curtains. From the yard, I waited for a long time, waiting to see some sort of movement. Then I called Dad. I was crying, defeated. I should have known better than to not get a key made to her apartment, I said between sobs. I'm just not good at this; I don't know what to do. I don't think I had cried out, pleaded to my father for guidance since I had been small. We were both surprised by my gushing. He was good at comforting me, however, and quickly reclaimed his position of parental mentorship and council. He told me not to worry. "She does this. It's probably because I talked with a woman at a retirement home the other day. I've been thinking it's time to look into such options, for the future. It was my mistake to tell her."

In rebellion, Grandma had decided to go into hiding. I contacted her landlord, who let me into her apartment; only her antisocial, but hunger-driven, cat greeted me. I scoured the city for days, calling everyone I knew she knew (about two people) and checking hospitals. My father made calls and promised to come to the city and search for her himself if she wasn't found after another few days. After a week, however, Grandma surfaced, saying she had just needed a break to think about things. What that meant, in reality, was that she had run out of money. She had been staying at the Red Roof Inn, living there and apparently frequenting a drag bar a block away, where they knew her by name and drink. "Gloria, hey, sweetie, the usual Bud?"

"Yes, doll." She turned to me, after introducing me to the bartender. "These boys are so nice, a bit confused, but they sure know how to have a good time."

The bartender returned with a Budweiser and a hotdog, which he said was on the house. I ordered a beer, too, at Grandma's insistence, but I was charged.

My father found out that Grandma had also been hanging out at the Red Roof Inn front desk, driving the workers crazy by pacing the lobby at night and smoking cigarettes, trying to make small talk with the clerk over coffee. This, I could only imagine—my grandmother is not capable of small talk.

"Jen," my father warned. "This little stunt was probably to get my attention, but it also means that your grandmother probably isn't taking her medicine. She's on an antipsychotic called Stelezine. The drugstore will give her a pill or two to hold her over until she gets a new prescription, but you need to get her into Dr. Bunker's immediately. The doctor has a way with words; she'll get your grandmother to take those pills."

I made her an appointment. She rode with me to Dr. Bunker's and periodically suggested that I drop her off at the airport or bus stop, asking first if she could please borrow some money. She just wanted to go visit some friends, she promised, she'd be back. I would ignore her until she grew indignant, crossing her arms. "You're out to get me, too. My own granddaughter."

"Grandma, I'm trying to help you. Don't you understand? I care. I looked for you when you ran away from me. I could have just said forget it, not pick you up at all."

"Oh, don't worry, you'll grow up eventually," she snapped. I gripped the wheel tightly, and we didn't speak for the rest of the drive. When we arrived, she said, "I still don't trust you, young lady. It's no wonder you don't have a fella." I thought about leaving her in the car. Maybe I could cash in on this appointment. I had some rage to work through. When I opened the car door, she surprised me by slamming it shut.

***

My visits to Grandma Gloria's apartment only seemed to get tougher because her moods were so unpredictable. I did notice that a cold Budweiser and a mentholated cigarette seemed to put her in a good mood. "I love that dizziness Budweiser gives me." And she didn't have any rules about not drinking in the morning or afternoon. Oddly enough (to me, anyway), she rarely drank more than one beer on any given day.

On good days, or with her Bud, she was beginning to charm me; her bad days, on the other hand, seemed to coincide with my own, and during these times I was combative. One day, as I waited for her to get ready, I overheard her talking to someone on the phone. "She'll abandon me. I can tell. That girl has no scruples. Something is wrong with her, and I just know she'll leave me. She's toying with me." She must have forgotten to whisper, I thought. I left the apartment, furious but quiet, so she wouldn't hear. I tried to ease down her hall steps, but they creaked. "Where are you going?" she yelled, just before I got in the car.

"I'm abandoning you, like you said."

"Come back here, sweet, please. I'm almost ready. I promise."

When I reentered her home, she offered me whisky. We called Dr. Bunker and cancelled the appointment that day, and, instead, we drank. She had one, maybe two. I had a bottomless china mug, which Grandma kept topped off. I could tell she used to be a damn good waitress. By late afternoon, Grandma and I had become fast friends; we were drunk. She told me stories about my father when he was young. Her stories were unlike his, she seemed to favor the past, casting a lovely sepia tone with her words, whereas my father's stories were sharper, more black and white. She taught me how to play canasta, and we laughed together as we played. I spent the entire day with Grandma; she made me toast in a skillet. "This is so you're not dizzy when you drive home," she explained. "Here, look," she showed me pictures of her mother, commenting that we looked alike.

Grandma reminisced about her mother, painting her as though she were a different person than the Glory I had heard about from my parents. I became enamored with my late, great-grandmother Glory. There was something about her picture that didn't add up to the stories I had heard. It was true that we share the same red hair, as opposed to the dark brown dominant in our family, and that our noses seem alike: thin and slightly long, dotted with freckles; our cheekbones look similarly high. She was a twenty-something year old woman in the photograph, and I recognized a familiar distraction in her eyes, as though she was waiting for what's next. Me, too, I thought.

When I picture Glory now, I imagine a girl like me, growing up in another time, a keenly dressed redhead, fifteen years old. She wears too much makeup, and her gloved hands settle defiantly on her hips. Her big dreams outweigh any good intentions; her idealistic, selfish nature, her downfall. This revised image is the result of a combination of genealogical research and imagination. The red hair, the age she ran away, the three marriages she left, the indignant behavior, unrealistic dreams, and, arguably, the narcissism are all true and verifiable. The rest I have to impose based on my own experience and what I can imagine it must have been like.

As I began to prod Grandma for more information about her mother, a mild obsession was forming in my mind. One day, when Grandma and I were out for our weekly pancake breakfast, this time at Bob Evans, she began a new story.

"You know, Mother left home the same way you did. Of course, she had better reason," she began. I ignored the slight and asked her to tell me more. "Mother told me she had never been so embarrassed. Grandpa had threatened to whip her in public and she grew so angry at Grandpa's threats that she began screaming at him in public. This was something no girl did to her father then," Grandma went on, sopping up some syrup with a spongy pancake.

"What did she do to get him so angry?"

Grandma explained that Glory's temper had flared when her father threatened to whip her for sneaking off with a man much older, an Army man.

"She was calling him weak and stupid. She disowned him, her own father! She hopped on a train and chugged off to a new life."

Grandma began to veer off subject, talking about how good Maxwell House coffee was, or some such thing, but I brought her back, begging that she tell me more. "Another day, Jen. I can't talk about Mother for too long right now. Later, though."

Laura

I heard a radio program announce that one out of every seven kids between the ages of ten and eighteen will run away, and I became distracted by the news, caught in a daydream—not a safe way to drive.

I looked in the rearview and made out a man with gray hair and sunglasses; he was mouthing something at me. He leaned on the horn again, and then a gap in the traffic opened up in the lane next to us. He drove around me, cutting in front of the CRX sharply, barely missing my bumper. There was a familiar fluttering in my chest, wings batting against my rib cage. My arms were heavy, my hands barely held on to the steering wheel, and I didn't trust my foot to stay on the gas. I gasped. *Panic.*

I realized that I wasn't driving like a normal person. My foot somehow couldn't push the gas pedal down hard enough, so I took a breath and said, "Looks like we have to pull over, Jimmy." I had named the CRX based on the fact that I could not get into it on the driver's side unless I crawled in *Dukes of Hazzard* style, through the window. I always felt as though I were breaking in. Paradoxically, the passenger's side door would not unlock from the inside, so I would provide a chauffeur-style service to anyone who wanted a ride. Grandma liked this, thought the action was voluntary.

I pulled the car into a safe parking spot and felt relief. Then, my chest went from fluttering to seizing, and I began having trouble breathing. I was scared to move, so I couldn't call for help. Just as suddenly as the fear sensation had arrived, it left. I felt attacked by it. I didn't know it at the time, but I had just had the first of many such panic attacks. Back then, I just figured I had a fatal disease, and I hoped to die at home, in my sleep, as opposed to publicly. Instead of dying, however, the feeling eventually lifted and I slept it off.

***

One of the things that Candice and I had bonded about was a disdain for marriage. She frequently recounted tales of mental and physical abuse endured during her first marriage. Ted, she always pointed out, was dispensable. And she liked it that way.

I was wary of and somewhat disgusted by men. At the same time, I had begun dating a lot. No, I wasn't promiscuous, but I went out on more than a few first dates. I would evaluate each man based on my terms: Men were potential partners, predators, or competitors. I had no friends, really, so women I just saw as the opposition. Everything I had acquired, even my friendships, I attributed to looks, and sexual energy; everything denied to me, the same.

My sexual confidence was lagging when I met Chris. I was misplaced, pathetic—I thought,—and I hated most men my age. One thing was for sure, when I first saw him—scrawny, dark Irish features, the perfect slope of a nose surrounded by a short goatee, milky brown eyes—the last thing I wanted from him was a relationship. And friendship wasn't an option.

Chris was a friend of my sister's. My sister and I had only recently begun a sort of friendship, and I found it odd that she began to invite me out often. We met up at Karaoke bars at night, thrift stores during the day. Chris was often there; I didn't realize that they had conspired to get me alone with him, so that he could make his shy advances, which I always refused or deflected.

During this time, I moved around quite a bit, worked different jobs, visited new bars. I was twenty-one now and I had one saving grace: I adored college, and I especially loved English courses. College had reminded me that when I was younger, I loved to read and write. Once, when I was seven, I had plagiarized a *Tom & Jerry* cartoon, presenting it to Dad on Father's Day as my own creation. In college, I learned to copy life.

I rarely spoke in class, or socialized. Instead, I wrote down anything I heard that sounded as though it may make a good line in a story or essay. Even the margins of my science and mathematics texts were littered with possible character outlines and sharp dialogue that I would think up or overhear. While this fed my newfound habit, I found out quickly that such extracurricular writing ruined any potential my textbooks had for resale. So I began to buy and fill notebooks.

I drowned in stories, spending long nights reading for class and writing papers; if there wasn't a paper to write, I wrote about other students or co-workers. I wrote with such fervor that I had little desire to do anything else. I even learned to mix my own White Russians at home. I had perfected the drink: equal parts Kahlua and Absolut 100 proof vodka, a dash of vanilla, a splash of skim milk, and one ice cube.

When summer came that year, I moved; my newest roommate had found love and subsequently shown me the door. Surprisingly, it was my sister who offered me a place to crash next, in exchange for grocery money and rides whenever she needed them.

***

Laura, my baby sister, took care of me. When I told her I hated my latest job at Adamsmark, another factory, where I sorted heavy uniforms onto different routing lines, my shoulders aching at the end of my six hour shift, she laughed. "You're going to set some kind of record for the most jobs a single person has had. You get hired so easily. It's probably because you look like a yuppie." My sister's style, at the time, could best be described as alternative. She was just beginning to acquire her now impressive collage of tattoos.

"I just need to find a job I like," I whined.

"You've been writing those stories a lot. I liked that one about the giant killer frogs, by the way. Try a bookstore." That moment, I mentally quit my job at the factory. The next day, I began to fill out applications at every bookstore within twenty miles of downtown Columbus. After a few disappointments and enough time to run completely out of money, I landed two interviews. One was at a mall bookstore, and the other was at a Barnes & Noble in a haughty neighborhood north of downtown. I decided that if I got either position, I would stick it out, no matter what.

I picked the store closest to my sister's apartment and decided I would work there. I was great at interviewing for jobs, great at bullshitting, I suppose. Only this time, there was something at stake. I arrived twenty minutes early. I sat in the parking lot, going over how I would answer interview questions: *What are your strengths?* Perseverance. *Weaknesses?* Hmmm…Impatience. *Why should we consider you for this job?* I am a hard worker. *What are your goals in life?* Getting out of my sister's house… no, wait…to graduate college and become an award-winning writer.

My immediate need for employment made me anxious in a way I had never been for an interview. I kept lighting cigarettes then putting them out and spraying myself with vanilla bean mist to cover the scent. Five minutes to nine I got a phone call. My sister's voice was full of jubilation. "We're getting a new snake, Jen, a ball python. Tim wants to sell it, and he said I could make payments. We're going to celebrate tonight. Chris will be there."

"Laura, that's really cool, but I can't talk. I'm getting ready for that interview at the bookstore. And I'm really fucking nervous."

"You *have* to get that job so that we can go out tonight, okay? Just think ball python and White Russians," she said, divinely.

Grateful for the distraction of comforting thoughts, I went in the bookstore smelling like burnt vanilla and no longer as nervous. I aced the interview, delighted, until we got to the last question: "What was the last book you read?"

With this, my mind went blank. Here, I did what I tended to do, I made up a story. "Um, it was a mystery novel, really action packed…I don't remember the name…it's the new one, by that woman." I waited for my interviewer, a compact woman with a long, brown braid, to fill in the blank. She allowed the silence. So, I peered over at the bestseller list and snapped my fingers. "There it is, *Tough Cookie*, the one with the picture of the cookie jar holding a gun. That was one fun book. I just read so many of those books that I can't remember the names sometimes."

"Oh, I do the same thing," she said, lighting up. "You're a big mystery fan?" I nodded, feeding my ridiculous lie. The last mystery I had read was a Nancy Drew title. "I love mysteries, too. I've never read Diane Mott Davidson, but if you say she's good, I'll have to check her out. Usually, I only read one of the bestselling authors. Do you read J.D. Robb?" Here, I told the truth. She went on. "Well, you should. You know it's a pen name; the author is actually Nora Roberts. Nora Roberts, the romance novelist?" I nodded. "She knew that the literary world wouldn't take her seriously if she tried to cross genres, so she picked that name, and fooled them."

"Smart," I said.

After receiving a few more book recommendations, I got a tour of the smallest bookstore I had ever been inside of. It was perfect. I was introduced to a handful of employees, each of whom seemed to have the same nervous way of nodding or saying hello then immediately going back to work without further conversation. When the manager extended her hand at the end of our meeting, I readied myself for the good news.

"Good to meet you, Jennifer. We'll check out your references and give you a call," she said.

She explained that they paid minimum wage, and that the position was competitive because college students loved to get discounts at bookstores; but she also said she had a good feeling about me and she'd check out that book I recommended. My heart pounded as I tried to remember which jobs I had listed on my application. One of them, I knew, had been Candice's salon. I had written Ted's name as the contact. What would he say about me? And what kind of manager calls references for a minimum wage job?

A week later, an unnamed python was feasting on a small white mouse in the kitchen. I liked to watch her eat, but I didn't like the fact that she had to do so often; mice were expensive and they smelled bad. We kept them in the fridge, next to the milk. I was telling Laura that she should give the snake back or else sell it when the phone began to ring, and surprisingly, she agreed. She got teary-eyed as she paced around the kitchen, watching her new friend, but early that day she had confessed that she had not become attached to this particular snake—there was something "detached about her personality."

"We can't afford her, anyway," I was assuring as I answered the phone.

"May I speak to Jennifer?" a prim male voice asked.

"This is her," I said, stomping my foot, to signal Laura. She looked up and smiled.

"This is Steven, from Barnes & Noble. Congratulations, Jennifer. The store manager really liked you, and your references checked out. We would love to offer you a part-time position here at our store."

"I would love to take one," I said, sounding a bit desperate.

"Great. When can you start?"

"ASAP," I said. I watched Laura pet her snake with her fingertips.

"Let's go with Monday, at nine," the man said. "Dress business-casual."

By Monday, the anonymous python was gone, Laura had a new iguana, which ate crickets and lettuce, and I was heading to my new job, the first job I would keep for an extended amount of time.

Years later, recently promoted to management at the bookstore, I had earned access to my file. When I found the original application I'd filled out, I noticed the change in my writing—it had been larger, loopier, and I found the interview sheet my hiring manager had used. It had a few lines for reference quotes, and I found only Ted's name. "Notes: 'Dependable.' 'Hard worker'" it said.

At the time, the mystery of how my references checked out did not go unnoticed, but I remember feeling relief, sure that she hadn't gotten through to Candice and Ted; I was grateful for this. My new position was sales, true, but it was different than any of the previous jobs I'd held. For starters, bookstore employees were mostly quiet and delightfully sarcastic; there was a healthy mixture of retirees, teachers, students and writers. What baffled me was the lack of turnover. Many of my co-workers had been at this store for at least a few months, many of them years, despite education level.

I spent most of my billable hours arranging books I intended to read, discussing books that I had read, and daydreaming. I had begun to adopt a common fantasy of booksellers, that of my future as a professional writer: martinis and money, travel and adoration—that rare sort of anonymous celebrity. I enjoyed the company I found at the bookstore, not only among co-workers, but also those I serviced, customers who shared my newfound passion for words. I was a newcomer to the vast literary world, and book lovers could sense it.

They offered me suggestions, eager to see what I would think about their favorite books. And I read voraciously, often at night in place of sleep.

With so much solitary work, my fantasies were large, but so were notions of the barriers I could see on my every side. It was here, during long hours at the store, between discussing books that my past began to surface in my mind. As I cleared dust from a self in the psychology section, I began to recognize certain titles. As I began listing these books, *The Bell Jar*, *One Flew Over the Cuckoo's Nest*, *Girl Interrupted*, *An Unquiet Mind*, and *She's Come Undone*, as my to-reads for summer, a regular customer recommended that I "branch out a bit." Yet many of these titles had stood out in my mind as recommendations from my past, my time spent at the adolescent rehabilitation center after I ran away. Once this memory surfaced others succeeded it. And I knew I had no choice; I began to indulge them, even write them down in a journal when I arrived home each day. It was odd how these scenes arrived so naturally and how little time had passed since much of it happened, yet with each scene, I felt removed from the girl who had lived through it.

At Laura's, I noticed that Chris had begun to show up more often. We played chess. We became friends, shared meals and ideologies. Slowly, he began showing me how a relationship was supposed to begin. Its subtlety was confounding—the courtship, the late-night phone calls and compliments, the small, romantic gestures. He was high-energy whereas I was slow-moving now, almost meditative; I liked the balance and I liked him, but I remained wary. Our relationship developed until we began comparing scars and telling embarrassing stories, and here I became frightened. So I decided to test the boundaries. I came out with it—my past, in a nutshell, which I laid out in detail over a few cappuccinos, a few dozen drinks, over the course of a few dates. This day was the first time I had really thought about the near past, let alone talked about it.

In response, Chris didn't pause. "You're like my dream girl. The bookish redhead with a sultry, sexy side."

"Stripping isn't sexy, it's business. It's dirty, gritty, capitalist exploitation," I explained.

"Whatever. You were just doing what you had to do. It's not like I'm perfect. I've got plenty to be ashamed of. We all have a past." I began to trust him. It wasn't long before we talked about moving in together.

Grandma called me, repeatedly, as I tried to enjoy a night with Chris, but he waited patiently as I explained to her that her neighbor was a nice old man, hardly capable of sneaking in her room at night and subjecting her cat to top secret government experiments. Chris's father had been schizophrenic, he told me after the call, and he understood. He understood a lot more than just that. I continued to take Grandma to her appointments, after which Chris would patiently listen to me grumble about my inability to understand her. Thankfully, he offered little advice. After all, what advice was there? He listened.

A few months passed and I was still working at the bookstore. I remember shelving romance novels one Sunday, a slow day, when a co-worker, Michael, rushed past me. I whispered to him to stop. He reappeared, resting his lanky frame, hip to shelf, and I took note of his agitated expression. His arms were full of books, but he waited as I allowed a calculated silence to linger between us. "What?" he asked.

"I just want you to be the first to know that this is my future," I said, pointing to the book I held. I mustered an authoritative tone and cleared my throat. "Now, I need you to listen. I've been masterminding the climax of my first book." I waited a moment then began, "She struggled against his masculine arms, but when he released her and she fell upon the bed there was no hiding the womanly expectation in her sea-green eyes. She, too, would soon be one of the undead." After stifling a chuckle, Michael shot me a sour look before shuffling off. "You have no future in vampire romance," I heard him say, laughing. I skimmed the pages and read a passage from the book I held, thinking he was probably right, but it was this day that things began to change. It was this book that wouldn't fall.

When I ended up in the ER, diagnosed with hysterics, I became more than embarrassed. "It is very likely I am going crazy, and if I get as bad as Grandma…," I told Chris, "You should look elsewhere for a nice, stable relationship." I paused a moment and added, "We can stay friends." Chris only laughed and assured me that he was willing to risk it. He had yet to see my panic in action and I had wanted to keep it this way. My room at Laura's was beginning to resemble the self-improvement section of the bookstore, laced here and there with a book on meditation, yoga, and breathing. I read every book I could find that promised to address panic, became hopeful that I could combat the pesky illness with a mixture of homeopathy, Buddhism, yoga, meditation, diet, and mantras. I tried it all, anything to prevent another attack, which doctors seemed to agree was inevitable.

Chris was treating me to grease-soaked quesadillas when my panic hit again. This time, it began with breath. I tried to remember my mantras and meditative techniques, but the thoughts of impending death bore down and worked to squeeze logical thoughts and structured techniques from my mind. Chris watched me shake. He was as helpless as I was, looking around frantically, moving to my side of the booth and stroking my back. He pushed my food away as though it were the cause.

"Take me home, get me out of here," I said between gulps of smoky air. When he reached for my hand to help me up, I became too confused to react. How do I move? What is the first step to extending an arm, pulling oneself upward to a standing position? I felt my legs shaking as I explained that maybe I wasn't ready to get up yet.

It wasn't a natural response for Chris to comfort. Instead, my panic seemed to reach to him and tap him on the shoulder. His voice became amplified as he asked me a succession of questions: "Will water help?" "Do you want and Advil?" "What should I do, Jen?" "You're not moving. If you want to go…." Finally, in desperation, he pulled me by the arm, instead acting from a place of worried frustration at my inability to answer his questions. "Are you really sick this time? Do you need an ambulance?"

I managed to ask him to take me home. He was eventually able to lift me from the booth and walk me to the car. That night, he held me carefully and told me what he'd seen as though I hadn't been there. I simply held his hand as my eyes traced shapes onto the plain gray walls.

"It was like you got this helpless look on your face," he said. "It was scary. I didn't know what to do." He said that maybe a trip away would help me, a vacation. I said I doubted it, but we could try.

Chris and I each put in requests for time off of work, and in August we embarked on a road trip to Yellow Springs, Ohio, an hour away from Columbus. It was a city known for Antioch College, where a person could get a bachelor's degree in "Self and Society," or some other generalized, self-defined curriculum that the student could map out and navigate as he or she saw fit. There were no grades, just pass or fail, which I found refreshing. The college intrigued me, and there was said to be a beautiful park next door to the campus where we had planned to hike.

When we arrived near campus, there was a protest of some sort going on. We pretended to be potential students and toured the grounds so that we could get a closer look. We were assigned a dreadlocked blonde guide who said very little as she showed us around. She vaguely pointed at certain buildings and explained what courses were taught where and by whom. The only building we got an in-depth view of was the English Department. All of the classrooms were set up with comfortable-looking chairs, situated in circles where workshops were held. I imagined myself there, my stories being discussed. The guide asked us if we wanted anything else, and then she walked over to the protest group, which consisted of about a dozen people.

We watched from the window. A few women paraded around with no shirts, proudly, holding signs that I did not read, nor care to read. I stared at these students. Chris stared at them, too. "Do you have any idea how much tuition is at this college?" he asked.

"It seems like a giant stage play," I said finally, ready to move on. "Any decent boobs out there?"

"Not really," he said, genuinely unimpressed.

We decided to hike on one of the mile-long trails in the park that bordered the campus. Rich, green maple trees and thick, summer heat fed our desire to succumb to the unabashed nakedness of Antioch. We stripped down to our underclothes as we ventured deep into the woods, stepping on helicopter seeds that fell from the trees. We found a waterfall that we could climb up to and walk through. The water was too cold for me, so I walked behind the falls and stood there, splashing water in Chris's direction until he joined me. At this point in the hike, everything was fantastic. We began kissing and wondering aloud what it might be like to live in Yellow Springs, which had only two downtown restaurants that we could find outside of the college. There were three bookstores on the same block, and, along with the campus, and the park, there was nothing but residential homes. We sat there a while as the mist from the falls sprayed our shoulders. It was all very sappy and surreal.

Then reality hit. We ventured off the path and got lost. Long after our hair dried out and the sun began to redden our skin, we found a dead end and had to turn around, but we must have headed in a slightly diagonal direction because we noticed, after a while, that the scenery had changed drastically.

The sun was dreadful and unrelenting, and I was growing irritable after we had been out there a few hours. We trudged along as though we had been walking for days. After a while, heading back, finally, in the direction we had originally come from, we didn't even care to find the campus anymore; we only wanted water, another waterfall. "Let's sit and rest," Chris said. He pulled out a pack of Camel Lights. "I wish I had my cell phone."

"I know. You already said that," I complained. "Let's *not* sit. We need to keep walking. I just want to get home, get the fuck out of these woods."

Chris wiped his forehead with his shirt, draping it over his shoulder. He climbed up on a rock and looked around. "Let's just keep going the same way," he said at last.

"No shit we're going the same way," I muttered.

"What?" he called out after me; I was walking briskly and I picked up my pace when I heard the edge in his voice. He ran after me and for a moment, I became scared. I felt him pull me backwards and then I felt his sweat-drenched arms wrap around my waist. Suddenly, I realized that the small ache at the bottom of my foot, which I had previously dismissed as a muscle strain, was, in fact, a blood clot. It would burst and I would die. My body went limp as I imagined Chris leaving me there, kicking the body or burying it under leaves so that he wouldn't be accused of something. But, as Chris's arms gently held me, I found myself able to breathe. He hugged me. "I'm sorry," he said. "I really didn't think this park was this big."

"I think I just had another attack," I said. "It was short, but…." Chris reached for my hand, and together we sat in silence until I was ready to continue.

Eventually, we found the open field that led to town. Once safely out of the woods, we fell to the ground in a heap. "I thought we were going to die in that forest," I said.

What happened next was nothing short of magic, movie-like in its unlikely perfection and fantastical romantic effect. As Chris and I savored our relief, each staring up at the clear sky, a mist, soft as flower petals began to fall over us, cooling our skin. I thought about the way my heart raced when Chris had approached me in the woods, and, as strange as this seems now, it wasn't until this day that I realized that the full extent of trauma from my past, which I had tried to drown in alcohol, was surfacing.

***

"We're moving in together," I told Mom.

"Have you thought about it?"

I explained that Chris and I had agreed to be allies, never to marry, to split all bills and chores down the middle, always to be honest. We were partners, friends, and we had decided to go at this world together.

After a silence, she laughed. "It's cute that you're calling me like this, asking for permission. It means you're nervous. Serious."

"I guess I want to know what you think about my decision. I mean…."

"Honey, I think it will work out fine." She laughed, as I began to pace my room. "You know this means you'll have to take care of his bird, right?" I sighed, told her I'd thought about this, and somehow I still wanted to take the plunge. "Your sister had a bird when you were young, you remember?" she asked.

"Yep. A Cockatiel."

"Do you know how much restraint it took me not to open a window and set him free?"

"Me, too. That bird was evil." Laura's bird had been a squawker—a constant annoyance, escaping his cage to squawk in my closet, leaving white pools of shit on my clothes.

"Well, this is a lesson for you. Love is about sacrifice," Mom went on. I could hear the metal scrape of her lighter. "How's my son-in-law doing, anyway?"

"He studies a lot. I think I should follow his example," I said.

Mom and Chris had become fast friends. They began talking on the phone—secret conversations in which they would ask each other how I had seemed lately. "Are Jen's panic attacks continuing? Is she making it to work every day? School?" Mom would inquire. Chris kept her informed.

Despite panic, my surroundings had changed rapidly with the transfer to a four-year college. I was making it to work almost every day, and college was far less challenging than I had thought it might be. Truly inspired by my boyfriend, I tried to take the opportunity seriously, so I joined the literary journal and made the tough decision to major in English instead of psychology. I had transferred with a plethora of stories that I wrote on breaks at work, and I turned them in to English professors who seemed eager to critique my work and compliment my off-beat plotlines and hard-edged characters, to see the dark places my imagination would wander.

Shortly after the move, I enrolled in a night course titled *The Dilemma of Existence*. It was taught by a spirited woman with a blunt-cut bob and trendy glasses who eagerly introduced me to Samuel Beckett, Franz Kafka, John-Paul Sartre, and Toni Morrison. I found the reading engaging, and the lectures inspiring and often perplexing. I found myself wanting to meditate on the arguments, unable to fully leave the classroom the way I did my other night courses—by running out of there and to my car, hungry for sleep.

Our last reading was Albert Camus. "Sometimes you just need a point of reference to gain clarity," Professor Banker said. I stared blankly after she introduced existentialism, wondering how pessimism could be taught through such a wide, honest smile. I rarely spoke in her class—none of the class spoke much—but my thoughts raced. I remember my chest tightening as she said, "Camus teaches us to make the most of a ludicrous existence."

Somehow, I felt as though Professor Banker had grabbed at some cord deep inside me and pulled at it one way then the next. I walked out of the classroom carefully, quietly. I drove home slowly. I hardly slept, but I lay still, watching Chris breathe. Was this really my life? I knew it wasn't. Running had felt more natural, and I knew I would run again—it was only a matter of time. Probably my life was ridiculous. Look at all the ridiculous shit I had done. I moved out to the front room and sat on the futon. I pulled the purple cover off the parakeet's cage and she immediately looked up at me, seeming annoyed.

Bird—Chris had named her aptly—lived behind the pale blue lines of her cage. Her home was adorned with beads and tassels that she pecked at with apparent joy. We thought it funny to decorate her cage, thinking the decadence seemed like a good idea; it was pretty, and the decorations gave her something to do. Chris and I could not have fathomed parenting an unfulfilled parakeet. I told him we were ready for more pets. What we didn't realize, as we continued to adorn Bird's cage with more and more beads, was that we might've have been making things harder for her.

We noticed that every three weeks or so a cycle began. Bird cuddled up to her beads (most often the purple ones with the hexagon shape) and ducked her head down under them so that they weighed heavy on her delicate back. From there she would lift her blue butt high into the air and bob up and down in a rhythmic motion. Whenever I caught her at it, I yelled at her to stop. She would stare past me through a small black disc of an eye, then resume.

A week or so after each encounter with the beads, three to five pink eggs would appear at the bottom of her cage. At this point Bird became less friendly and rarely sang. She began fanning her tail above her eggs and gyrating for hours on end to keep them warm. Eventually, she would come to the realization that her plastic lover was no replacement for the real thing. Beads know nothing of how to father, and as Bird realized this she would stop singing, and seemed dour. Her demeanor stayed this way until, ultimately, she took her anger out on the source of her discontent.

Her pointed beak would go to work on the pink eggs, breaking them open to reveal nothing; a symbol of her inadequacy. Then a week or so would pass before Chris or I would catch her with that butt hiked up once more.

Albert Camus believed all of life to be absurd, that existence is purposeless. He taught that freedom lies within our minds, our ability to add purpose to our lives, giving each person an amazing amount of control, responsibility. People live to push a perpetual rock up a perpetual hill until they die. I would sit in class, my ears filled with the heavy air, my chest tightening, my breath growing short. Another attack, difficult to ride out. I had been pressing the table in front of me with my palm, pressing hard enough that it hurt when I gripped the wheel driving home. I was able to wait the panic out now, able to remember my breath.

"Maybe we should take her to a veterinarian," I told Chris as we watched Bird poke holes in lifeless yolky eggs. We didn't know if a bird was capable of fury, but we agreed that she seemed to exude it. We agreed to remove the beads.

Bird was in a cycle of determination towards pain, destruction, and temporary resolve. Her cycle always seemed disheartening, but nothing compared to the pain we inflicted when we decided to "quit torturing her" and remodel her cage. I was met with the fury I had seen earlier. Bird began to peck at her empty cage voraciously. She squawked a high-pitched rant at my audacity. "Maybe you should put the beads back on," Chris said. I wasn't sure.

The marketing agency that packaged the beads as "Endless Parakeet Entertainment" may not have had sex in mind, but Bird had found unwavering entertainment in an altogether existentialist way.

I handed the beads to Chris and told him to do it himself. To me, it seemed mean, as though feeding her fantasy; only in the end, this would perpetuate more pain. He re-adorned her cage with the beads and we sat together, watching, as she began to sing. I began to mix a drink, asking Chris if he'd like one. "I have to go to school tomorrow morning," he said. I poured the vodka back in its bottle and picked up two five pound weights, which I curled until my biceps felt bruised.

Family

Grandma had been calling me a few times daily for a ride to the mall or a few dollars to get some more cat food; I would show up at her apartment, a thirty minute drive, and find her cupboards stocked with cat food. I would get angry and storm out, only to sit in the car for a moment and then go back to apologize for yelling and leaving so abruptly. This was our cycle: I would worry then grow resentful, which would be followed by expressions of anger, guilt and then profuse apologies; meanwhile, she would complain about people who followed her or practical things—how her granddaughter treated her "like an orphan." I suppose we were going through that awkwardness that comes from mutual shame and our varied forms of anxiety.

When Grandma was having one of her breaks, she would call, panicked, and with new resolve I would listen, ask questions, and look for patterns in her vague answers. I told her everything was fine, she just needed to go to sleep. Often, she would call me the next morning and neither of us would bring up the previous night's conversation. After a while, I began to see my grandmother's illness as a mystery, a code that I might crack. I began to write the things she said during our late night conversations. *Who was following her? Always a woman, always unnamed. What was the antagonist's reason for following Grandma? Jealousy. Other consistencies: Breaks always happen after simple decisions, often her choice of dinner meat. When did it happen? Usually at night, early in the morning. Who could help? The Navy. Always the Navy.* "Call the Navy, Jen, please; they'll know what to do."

***

Grandma and I sat the booth closest to the door of the Waffle House. I was telling her about my raise to full-time at the bookstore, where I would be making eight dollars an hour! I got past my probationary period. She told me she didn't like her medication anymore.

"Dad says you had better start taking your Stelezine again," I said. She dodged the argument swiftly, explaining that *her* grandmother was suspicious of medicine for good reason, and that I should be, too. My great-great-grandmother would not go to a doctor for anything. Her reason, Grandma explained, was that she had seven children who needed her at the house and she couldn't risk getting sick from some doctor's office.

"Oh, those kids were all so beautiful," Grandma said, sidetracked again, as though she were picturing her mother and aunts' pictures as children. She scooped a forkful of pancake into her mouth. We had been at breakfast for a while; she seemed at peace when she talked about the past. "Well, all but one—Aunt Jo was not attractive at all! But the rest of them, oh! They were the most beautiful kids around," Grandma said again. And again she took a bite. She compartmentalized people by their beauty or lack thereof. She made sure to tell me that I *could* be beautiful if I tried harder—if I knew how to comb my hair properly, or dress suitably, or wash my skin with the right soap. She continued, "I think that if I had seven beautiful children like that, I wouldn't want to leave the house, either. But it was a pity. She eventually became fearful of everything outside of her own home."

"She was agoraphobic," I said.

"What? What's that? No. She was just distrustful, and for good reason." Grandma looked appalled by my comment; her face seemed to say it was a wonder anyone leaves home, ever, as though it was a wonder we were out now.

"Labels are just more specific now," I said. "To be agoraphobic is not a weakness, but an illness."

Grandma pursed her lips, outlining the inaccuracy with which she applied her cherry lipstick that morning. She was getting defensive. "Labels are useless. You either have a good reason to stay inside or you go outside to do what you have to do." This, I have to admit, makes a lot of good sense.

I watched as Grandma fought each her labels stridently—schizophrenia, obsessive-compulsive disorder, paranoid personality disorder, depression, hysteria, melancholia, and more. Our day together was one of her good days, so far. Going out to eat was arduous. Some days she felt her choice of pancakes over eggs or white toast over rye meant the world would soon end or the war would escalate, because of her faulty decision. This day, she spent ten minutes deciding what to order, and while she had displayed no obvious regrets yet, I was waiting.

Grandma Gloria, at age eighty-four, had finally agreed to move into a retirement center. My father made the arrangements, and *forgot* to tell them that she had been diagnosed with a mood disorder that required medication. Any place that catered to such special needs charged at least double what this place did. As it was, she had to sign over everything she had to live her last days in this place, which looked remarkably like my first apartment.

The space she lived in was small, cave-like. There was a front room and a dining/kitchen area that led to a bathroom. The first time I visited, I wasn't surprised to see her room was filled with upside-down furniture, and most of it was covered in flour. I was expecting something;

admittedly not this, but by this time, she would have to work harder than that to catch me off guard. I asked her why she arranged the room the way she did. She said it was to protect her things and that the flour was there to record prints, in case anyone broke in. "Like they always do."

I offered to help her clean up the flour that day, and she asked me what I found so dirty about it. "It's just flour," she said. I shrugged and kissed her goodbye. She asked me if I wanted to use her hairbrush before leaving, to look more presentable. I said I did not.

"Thanks anyway, Grandma," I said.

After a few minor incidents, Grandma expressing her desire to leave, referring bitterly to the home as her "final destination," she began to assimilate in an unforeseen and amazing way. She found friends, explaining that this was the first time in a long time that she had neighbors who were always home, people she could visit at all hours and discuss the old days with. One woman, in particular, became a close friend of hers, and she insisted that we meet.

"This here is Dottie," she said as we entered a room directly across the hall from my grandmother's. Dottie was confined to a wheel chair that was adorned with a drink holder and purple arm rests. She was hunched, shaking subtly. She was eighty-nine years old, and standing beside her my grandmother appeared the epitome of youth and vigor. Grandma, with her freshly-dyed hair the color of wet clay, kissed her gray friend on her colorless cheek, leaving a red smear. "We just get along so well, don't we, Dottie?"

"Oh, yes. When I met your grandmother, it was as though we'd known each other our whole lives." Dottie asked me if I could lower the volume on her TV. She was watching a critical report about the No Child Left Behind program, which Laura Bush was defending.

"That woman is married to the devil," Grandma observed. Dottie, one of the few liberal-minded residents, and a proud equal rights activist in her day, had laughed agreeably with this comment. As the two women discussed the eminent danger our country was in under Bush Jr.'s reign, my grandmother's insights, many of which I found extreme, were perceived by her friend as astute.

"They have control over everything," Grandma moaned. "You can't trust a soul. I'm even scared to eat on Thursdays, what with the way they tamper with our food."

"Grandma," I sighed.

"No, dear, your grandmother is on to something there. Our food industry is downright evil. Why, I just read an article the other day about trans fats and what they are doing to our kids."

Happily, I reported Grandma's progress, her friendships, and improved mood to my father when we spoke. "Your Grandmother has a way of charming people. People that aren't family, that is," he said.

He was pleased, relieved to hear that her delusions hadn't gotten her into any trouble yet. Occasionally, over the course of the next year, my father would get phone calls from the resident night manager, who would report that my Grandmother was roaming the halls, trying to spread her prophecies of doom, but for the most part, she seemed happy. The regular interaction was good for her, and she even seemed to be taking her medicine regularly.

In my personal war against panic, I had adopted a methodical breathing technique that always seemed to be forgotten with onset of the attack. I had investigated more specific therapies than yoga and meditation, booking appointments for reiki, nutritional therapy, hypnotherapy, and finally a sort of sound therapy that was referred to as the vortex treatment, which was eighty dollars for an hour of lying in an elevated bed surrounded by metal tubing that was said to transfer and trap the sounds of therapeutic rhythms, sending them to my body, balancing my own rhythms. I kept an open mind. Unfortunately, the panic persisted, still arriving at ridiculously tranquil times.

By the end of the summer, I was beginning to think myself insane. I found myself in the ER again shortly after my vortex treatment, which I had briefly thought to have cured me. I was unable to breathe or find the right pressure on the gas pedal of the car. I drove myself to the emergency room this time, choosing not to call anyone until the doctor verified that I was, this time, really dying.

After hours of waiting and a few minutes with a doctor, I was released with another psychologist referral. At this point, I had no choice. "Don't do it," Chris warned, with Laura nodding along behind him. "Everyone I know who has tried those antidepressants has either become crazier or lethargic. Believe me."

I thought I'd take half of what was prescribed, try it out, but I didn't tell anyone. The prerequisite for this was a psychiatrist, so I asked the psychologist I was seeing to recommend someone. I explained that I couldn't wait.

Second Diagnosis

The words Medication Management were embossed on the door. It was the last link in the chain of recommendations I received since my first diagnosis. The psychologist had recommended this place, and though I had initially rebelled, I ended up making the appointment during a two-week bout of intermittent panic and insomnia. The panic seemed to be adapting to the meditation and breathing techniques I'd armed myself with. I was desperate.

After inviting me inside her office, the doctor apologized for her lateness, plopped into her seat and began shuffling papers around on the glass table in front of her, never looking up at me. She was not dressed like most doctors; she wore jeans and a flower print shirt that tightly hugged her large breasts and the rolls of fat below them. I stood there wondering why I was there until she motioned toward a brown and purple couch. She said there was some paperwork I would have to fill out and then she leaned over the table to hand me a clipboard with two sheets of paper attached.

"These are diagnostic tests," she said.

One paper inquired about my sleep patterns and tendencies toward thoughts of doom. The other one was a column of checkboxes labeled Goldberg Mania Quiz. I crossed my legs, squeezing them together as I marked true next to the question about disrupted sleep patterns and false next to one inquiring about suicidal attempts. Does the number of trues a person checks determine the degree of her mania? I wondered. When I finished, I looked down at the blue circles I made with my pen, noticing that I marked more trues than falses. I handed the clipboard back to her tentatively. She asked me questions about my childhood, then my tendency to make irrational decisions—this was redundant, since it had also been one of the test questions. I began confiding in her.

"I'm edgy, and I can't sleep. I've been restless a lot in the past, but my life is good now. I want to get over it." She nodded. I told her a few stories about past experiences that led me to believe I was prone to regular depression. Meanwhile, she took shorthand notes. There wasn't anything subtle about this woman, including the fact that she intermittently looked up at the clock. Whenever her eyes veered toward the wall where the clock was perched above me, I would stop talking and look with her, wondering how much insurance money was being spent per minute as I recounted my youth on her plush couch.

"Okay, so you ran away when you were fifteen; you've made a lot of impulsive decisions," she began as though she was making a simple calculation. Runaway plus impulse plus insomnia equals what? "We need to move on," she said.

I began to wriggle my foot, shaking it up and down so that my thigh jiggled. It was time to leave. This woman had no interest in me. She was ready to move on, and I didn't trust her. When I began to look around as though I would leave, she asked me if I was on any medications, and began to inquire about my general health. I told her I was generally healthy.

After excusing herself for a few moments, sitting down in front of a computer, she asked me my address and phone number. She asked me if I wanted to set up a credit account so that she could automatically deduct each session we have from my account. I declined this service. She explained her semi-conclusive diagnosis: "You seem to have a generalized anxiety and some depression." She had that right, but I had yet to hear what she would say next. She explained that based on some of the stories I told, there was a possibility that I had cyclothymia, which is a mild version of bipolar disorder. "Something we should watch for signs of," she had said, rubbing her eyes. She gave me a sample bottle of pills, explaining that there might be mild nausea at first, but side effects were usually temporary. "The antidepressant will help you to sleep eventually," she said. "This is a new medication. And I think it'll be a good start for you."

Much to my surprise, she handed me another sample bottle and said, "Now, *this* prescription is to help you sleep *right now*. I'll only give you ten of these." They were sleeping pills. I hadn't asked for the sleeping pills, although one of my main complaints had been a lack of sleep. Pills like these came with the warning: highly addictive. She's a drug dealer.

"The antidepressant will take a while to kick in," she said, "so don't stop taking them if you don't see immediate results. In the meantime, you should see a counselor."

The doctor went on to explain that she wanted to see me monthly for a while to monitor the progress of the medication and to make sure I didn't have cyclothymia, but not to worry, these sessions would only be fifteen minutes long and would not include any more of my life story. She said she didn't do "talk sessions." I understood. This was *Medication Management*. We had to keep things status quo. Instead, she gave me a business card. This day, I resolved to do whatever I had to do to get mentally fit.

***

As I began my own therapy, I watched as my grandmother began to respond to a new medication. Her psychologist was invested; she seemed to approach Grandma as a sort of diagnostic mystery. She called me, asking about Grandma's behavior, but her tone was hardly clinical. It was only a matter of time before Grandma became less of a case study and her psychologist began referring to her as a friend.

I had continued to dine weekly with my grandmother, even though her doctor now offered to pick her up. Grandma's madness rarely peeked through this temperate time; when it did, it was usually late at night. When I would speak to her, listening to her predictions and assurances that the world was breaking apart, piece by piece, I wanted to understand where each thought began. I envisioned her delusion as a tree that had roots deep in the brain, the irrationality branches farthest from its trunk. I had begun to believe what my father did, that we could beat this thing.

The two of us would discuss how we might be able to influence Grandma's behavior by refusing to coddle her delusions. "Make her angry," Dad would say. "Start an argument with her about something. Sometimes this will distract her from her thoughts. She gets angry and her head clears." We conspired. My father and I became co-conspirators. For a short time, I began to record what Grandma said when she was particularly delusional, and then study it alongside my homework. I signed up for psychology courses at college and tried to apply what I learned, but eventually I realized that there were no real patterns. As my panic attacks continued, I began to lose hope. I was thankful for our shared mission, our burgeoning friendship, but it didn't take long for my father's idealism to wear away my own anxieties, my ability to relate, if only in my own pathetic way. I felt helpless myself; how could I help her?

Her deep-set green eyes seemed to know that I understood her position, the way they grabbed my gaze as she tried to tell me what went on in her mind. "Jenny, it's just terrible," she would say. "No one knows, and it's so lonely."

"Know about what, Grandma?" I'd ask.

"The whole thing," she'd say mysteriously, "everything's just falling apart." Conversations like this would go on and on. Grandma's dilemma to put her fear into words was something I could relate to, and thoughts of her own helplessness would often visit me in the midst of panic. "Tell me more about Glory," I'd always ask.

"Mother?" she'd ask. I'd nod, eagerly, feeling approximately six years old again.

When Grandma spoke of her mother, it was as though Glory had been movie star, a representation of glamour and strength, but never love, never in the sense one usually speaks of one's mother. Grandma always seemed to be longing to know her better, know her mother through reexamination of memory. But her mother, it seemed, was only an image, a mirage.

"Mother left, just like you," she once said. It was that conversation at breakfast that began my fascination with Glory. "She was a very beautiful woman. She used to turn down men left and right. You know if you only left your pretty curly hair alone, combed it out, you, too, could look just as beautiful."

"Um, thanks."

"Oh, you'd have to take care of that skin, too. Mother had porcelain skin. She never let those freckles pop out like you do. And she had much better taste. I bet you drove the boys wild yourself, though. Even with that straight, limp hair."

"I did drive them crazy, I guess."

"You two both left your father." Grandma added, squeezing my hand. "You only come see me as an obligation. I feel so abandoned." Was this her way of saying that I, like Glory, left her, too? That I, like Glory, was never really there for her in the way I was supposed to be?

Glory and I were the same. When I think about her leaving her father, I imagine myself. She was a few months older than I was when I left, but she must have had common motivation. Her longing must have come from somewhere. She was misunderstood, probably in pain, not as hardened and cold as I had been led to believe as a child.

Glory was fifteen, close to sixteen years old when she ran away. Grandma said that she was addicted to the notion of making it big in America. Chicago was booming, beckoning to those with big dreams and quick feet, so she fled her traditional household in Montreal and made her way on the first train she could find. Her goals were simple: find a rich man to marry and put his money to work. The men of her dreams were said to be cavalier, well-dressed, smart, and, most importantly, rich. WWI had ended and the American Dream was there for those actively seeking their fortunes.

Sixteen year old Glory Watson, a runaway from Canada, became Glory Hale, marrying Gilbert LeRoy Hale, my paternal great grandfather, who provided her with American citizenship, two children, and her first household. The couple separated shortly after he lost all his money in 1929 in the stock market crash; their divorce was final in 1933. Glory still craved money and excitement, and it didn't take long before she realized that her two small children were a heavy weight. Hearsay says that it was around this time that Glory reconciled with her parents and left her children with them.

One year later, she moved to Pennsylvania and became Glory Grove. Her new marriage lasted approximately ten years. One year before her second divorce, in 1944, Glory enlisted in the Women's Army Corp. She began working as a Packing Case Maker, and her year in active service led to a new feeling, one that was sweeping women across the United States. The feeling of self-reliance, Grandma tells me, may have been a factor in her mother's second divorce.

Glory's code seems to be as difficult to crack as Grandma's. A few things just don't add up. Upon finding Glory's military records, for instance, I was confused to find her "Nativity State or Country" was Washington D.C., but I couldn't find any record of her living there. Likewise, on a census form, she had claimed her birthplace to be "England," another location in which I found no record of her residence, let alone birth. Was she delusional or merely a compulsive liar? Glory took a few years off of marriage, living on her second husband's alimony and traveling, searching for investment opportunities. She married for the last time in 1952 in New York, only to divorce for the last time in 1957.

With and without husbands, Glory insisted that she take long trips with her friends, avoiding motherly duties so that she could maintain her composure. According to Grandma, she never admitted fault for leaving home. "She had a lot of pride and she knew what she wanted."

Until her death in a small retirement home in California, a few days before Christmas in 1992, she continued to travel, seeking her fortune. She visited, but never spent enough time to establish a relationship with her grandson (my father) or other extended family members, outside of asking for a place to stay for a night. Something was propelling her forward, repelling her from us. She had begun buying properties late in life, finding her knack for real estate investing.

***

I know the insatiable tug of the world outside of what I knew, how the world becomes small when I lived one place too long, my schooling, my house, predictable days. Perhaps Glory had found the answer. She must have thought that there was something better for her, and if only she had more freedom, more money, she could find it. The way I remember my own thoughts, they were similar, though not stated.

***

I know what it is like to feel restless and anxious and too proud to go home, to blame the world for something that feels innate. I know what it's like to want to start over. Unlike my great grandmother, I didn't dream of great fortune, nor did I travel very far when I left, but I did share grandiose expectations of finding a different life. I remember thinking that if I left my father, if I had the freedom to do what I wanted to do, I could achieve anything.

It wasn't just my father I was leaving. I was leaving a lifestyle. Our neighborhood was rough. Gangs were glamorized at school and the popular kids were the ones with the most expensive tennis shoes. If someone who was not popular wore expensive tennis shoes, that person would be beaten and left barefoot, and the next day one of the popular kids would have a new pair of Nikes.

I didn't have to worry about losing my shoes, but the climate at school made it hard for me to breathe. My friends were poor and my aspirations were petty. Make more money and buy things to show that money off, I thought, just never buy expensive shoes. I enjoyed skipping school and drinking behind the mall downtown, smoking Newport Kings and walking around my neighborhood, pretending to be tough, dressed in baggy clothes—before I ran away, I was a girl who knew better than to wear anything tight.

Looking back, I remember believing that life in any other neighborhood, at any other high school, with any other family, would have been better. I believed that I had to run away to find that beautiful life that existed outside. I wonder whether Glory felt this way, too. Maybe she was acting out selfishness and calculated motives, but somehow I think there was more to it. I believe she was tortured in some way. Maybe she blamed her parents and her surroundings for her pain, the same as I did.

I had been thinking about leaving home for months before I left. When I finally did it, the knowledge that I couldn't go back was instant. I don't know what Glory found after she left, other than the information I could find from her personal records: her marriages; her child's and grandchildren's vague and imaginative memories. Could things have been more complicated than they are on paper and in hearsay? I wonder what the world had in store for a girl on her own, fleeing to Chicago in the twenties. She was, after all, just a girl. What I found in the nineties was a world that seemed to force me into the pool head-first and dare me to sink. Like Glory, I just continued to run.

Adaptation

My father called me and said he'd be in town in a few days. It was only months from graduation and we planned to celebrate at the Olive Garden. He wondered if it would be okay if he slept on my futon for a night. "Of course," I said. He had a list of things he wanted to do: take a jog around Antrim Lake the first day, maybe go up to Sharon Woods on the second and get some ice cream at Graeter's, like we used to. Did I remember their Buckeye Blitz ice cream? He wanted to check out the bookstore where I worked. Did I know how proud he was of me for keeping a job? And then he suggested that maybe the two of us could call Laura and visit for a while. Maybe go see Grandma. "Of course," I said. "All of the above."

Weeks earlier, Dad had woken up in his Massachusetts bathroom unaware of how he got there. He didn't remember having two daughters. He didn't remember being married or living in Massachusetts. He didn't remember his middle name. He'd had a TIA, Transient Ischemic Attack, often referred to as a mini-stroke or a warning stroke. He had chosen not to worry me with the news. My stepmother had called to tell me about the incident; he had chosen to spare me the details, she'd explained. But he was recovering when she called.

I remember that phone call, the distance I had felt between us evaporating in the silence. I could see my father's face in the car as I merged onto the freeway at thirty miles an hour, his struggle toward patience and understanding. I could see him, younger, after I ran away. He sat in the same CRX, across the street from the teen center two weeks after I'd left. I had gone with James to visit my friends, and I thought I had glimpsed Dad's profile, his chunky sunglasses and beard. He was watching over me. At the time, I made sure it didn't look like I had spotted him, but he had already chosen to let me be. It had been only a glimpse, but his agony had transcended sight, etched details onto his face from such distance. Later, he'd told me that it was that day, while he watched me from across the street, finally found his little girl that he knew that he had to let go and allow me to come back on my own. I may have been locked out, but all I ever needed to do was ask for the key. I knew that, right? I said that I did.

I wanted to know what this must have felt like for my father in that instant. A man with no memory of who he is must feel fear, I thought, and I adopted his memory as my own: an image of self in the bathroom mirror; the grasping desire he must have felt, the way he must have struggled to add a definition to that self, to own it. I imagined him

171

releasing this desire. This was something more abstract than panic, and I wanted to relate so that I could help him.

"I've been having panic attacks," I confided, partly expecting reciprocal confidence. "I tried something called Paxil, but I began to panic, worry it might cause an aneurism or something."

My father had begun to practice yoga then, along with aerobics and weightlifting classes at the gym by his apartment. And he insisted I begin yoga. When I said I was practicing, he said that I wasn't doing it enough. Physical health means mental health, he'd told me. We jogged around the same trails we used to when I was a kid. As we ran, I felt the gravelly trail kick up under my feet and lengthened my stride. Since my panic attacks began, I'd quit smoking and gone on a sort of health kick myself, so I was up to the challenge. We went from a light jog to a run, until Dad broke away the last leg, sprinting to the end. I sprinted, too, to catch up, but hardly made a dent in the space between us.

When we were finished, we stretched and I complimented my father on his infuriatingly good health. "Maybe *I* should take an aerobics class," I said, huffing.

"You should. They really work you. You should've seen how much I struggled at first. That class went so fast; a bunch of twenty-something year old girls and me." He laughed.

"That's to be expected," I said. After the run, I offered to show Dad where I worked.

The two of us walked around the bookstore, talking a little too loudly. I introduced him to co-workers who smiled and shyly looked back to their tasks after shaking my father's hand. Regular customers glared from their comfy chairs as I told Dad that after graduation I was thinking about moving. He said it would be good for me to start over. When I went to buy something from the café, I heard my father humming along, loudly, to the music that was playing. This humming was intermixed with irritable sighs from those regulars. When I returned with his mocha he was still at it. Another customer, incensed, collected his things and moved from his chair. He pushed by me and I smiled at his anger. I found it ridiculous. I began to hum along, too.

***

I didn't go my college graduation, but I didn't have to. Instead of waiting, seated in fold-out chairs for my name to be called by robed academic advisors, I sent them all thank you cards and arranged some coffee dates, and spent the evening of commencement at my mother's dinner table. I cut into four thick layers of cheese that had melted seductively against homemade meat sauce and thick, tender noodles: Mom's lasagna. Chris, Laura, and I sat at the table as Mom bustled around the kitchen, telling us that she had two kinds of cake and a cherry pie for dessert. She was radiant, her olive skin tone against a gentle moss green, and her hazel eyes lined with purple. "You look beautiful today, Mom." My mother responded by bucking her head back before uttering a purposefully careful thank you. To say that my mother was surprised by the simplistic compliment would be too shallow. I believe her tentativeness, even shock, at my observation was revelatory. It was here I realized how long I'd failed to notice her beauty, but that I was noticing it now was hardly a reflection of my own coming of age. Rather, my observation was possible because I could see my mother's fledgling pride, not in my accomplishments, but in her own. She'd somehow, beneath my limited gaze, found peace. She placed a ceramic bowl of iceberg lettuce in front of me, a bowl destined to be ignored, and kissed my cheek.

"Jen, way to use your noodle," Laura said and with a flick of the wrist, flung a large noodle at me. I ducked, but it stuck limply to my shoulder.

"How the hell did you do that?" Mom said. "You flung that noodle like it was a Frisbee."

Laura gave a slow shrug, suggesting mysterious ways.

"You're wasting good noodles," I said and peeled it off slowly, holding it up to my mouth as though I would actually eat it. "What did you do anyway, suck it clean?"

She laughed as I flung it back, missing. I found myself chasing my sister out Mom's front door and into the yard. A neighbor watched. I had picked up the noodle and now it was dangling from between my finger and thumb. I held it up, shaking it at my sister. I flung it back and missed. The neighbor, a timid gay man named Henry, who would sometimes smoke cigarettes with Mom on the front porch and bitch about his boyfriend, looked at us as though we were gaudy lawn ornaments. We both waved at him and laughed.

"Aren't you glad you're part of the family now?" Mom was asking Chris as we walked back in.

"I am," he said, genuinely as he shoveled rich forkfuls of his dinner into his mouth. Mom and I locked eyes.

After dinner, Chris said that he had an announcement.

"Well, I got an offer." My mother hollered with joy. She hugged him and then me. "There's a catch. Um...."

"Spit it out," Laura said.

"We'd have to move. I...I mean, I'd have to move. I want Jenny to come with me, but it's up to her. Do you, um, want to?" I smiled with one half of my mouth, the way I do when I'm asked a ridiculous question. "Get out of Ohio? Hell, yes," I said. "Hell, yes!"

"The job is in Texas." I stopped smiling. "In San Antonio." I would be following this man across the country. My mind ticked off scenarios: Job, I could transfer; Grandma, safe, in a home and with regular care and medical treatment; my sister; Mom. She looks thrilled with her new son-in-law—she knew it long before I would. "Are you sure you don't want to think about it first?" I thought about the pang of sickness I felt when I drove downtown, past my old house. When I would encounter regular customers from the club at the mall and would have to avert my eyes—to which they often responded, "Georgia! Hey! When I would patronize one of the many stores and restaurants I'd worked at a few weeks, only to AWOL from. I had felt, if not ashamed of, burdened by my past and I was ready to leave it where it belonged.

The psychiatrist Grandma visited every other week had offered to come visit her at her retirement home weekly, relieving me of my duty. I had put off telling Grandma I was leaving, but to she didn't take it nearly as hard as I had thought.

"I'm leaving, Grandma, but I'll visit a lot. I promise."

"I knew you'd leave," she said. "My family always leaves." Grandma offered me some coffee. I accepted before I realized that she was making instant coffee. I watched as she dumped an unmeasured pile of coarse brown crystals into a pot of boiling water. She stirred the muddy mixture, judging it for color, and then added more crystals.

"You really do remind me of my mother." When she said it I must have looked distressed because Grandma considered my face and added, "Oh, my mother was a beautiful woman. She gets a bad rap."

"She abandoned you," I added, lifting a dainty pink mug to my lips where the liquid's acids seemed to bite at my nose. I lowered the mug.

Grandma smiled as she poured herself a mug then abandoned the pot and pulled out a package of cookies. "I like this kind. Any kind of cookie with that elf on the package, that's how you know you have a quality cookie." She said this with resolve. I told her there was a smudge of lipstick on her teeth and she double checked the situation by scrutinizing her smile in the reflection of a fork. She still had her own teeth; they were Dijon colored, stained with seventy plus years of use.

"Grandma, can you tell me more about Glory?" She didn't hear me. She placed an entire cookie on her tongue and closed her lips around it, holding it there as she placed two more cookies on the table in front of me. "Grandma, are you saying I'm leaving you like your mother?"

"My mother had a lot going on. A woman then, with her drive, had a lot to contend with, but she really *was* something. You like talking about her, don't you? She always wanted to be moving, and, boy, did I miss her when she wasn't around."

"How old were you when she left?"

"Eight. My Grammy took care of me. But mother would visit, and when I did see her we had the best talks! *We* should have those talks, you know, but we don't. You're always too busy." I chose to ignore the jab.

"Do you think that's why she ran away from her parents? Because she felt restless, like she had to move?" I wanted to apologize for her. Could this panic be guilt?

"Oh, yes. She had big dreams, but she was also very determined."

"And *you*, you think I'm like her?" I asked.

Grandma laughed. "In that restless way."

I heard the pot boil and ran to it. Grandma ate another cookie. As I refilled her mug with chalky coffee, she pushed my hair off of my shoulder. "You know, my mother knew how to style that pretty red hair. She didn't ruin it with an iron like you."

"Do you think you could tell me more about her on the phone?"

"I have gobs of stories about Mom. Did I tell you she was in the military?" When Grandma said this, I noticed her voice lifted. She admired her mother; seemed to remember more of Glory than the crotchety and careless old woman, the unfit mother, the predatory wife, the estranged great-grandmother. I told Grandma that I was eager to unearth these stories, and I promised to call and visit often. "I'm sure I'll have stories for you soon, too," I said. Stories I would tell.

She walked me outside and stopped just short of my car. "Just remember, Jenny, you have to be careful. You look for trouble, you'll find it."

When we parted I was close to tears. I considered my grandmother's dark auburn hair—a new color courtesy of a new visiting cosmetologist at the residency—and her crisp frilly blouse and blue pants pulled up to her bust. "I'll miss you, Grandma," I called out, waving from the car. She stood only a few feet away.

"I'm used to being the orphan," she yelled. "Everyone runs out eventually."

Instead of feeling my fists clench, I nodded. I thought about what she said and what I was running from and how it had clung while everything around me moved, so that only the view had changed. I thought about my family, its scattershot and awkward togetherness, and I walked back to my grandmother, kissed her on the cheek, leaving a trace of gloss. "I'm not leaving you," I said.

What I meant was that I wasn't running. And it was true. I hadn't been running for a while, and it had dawned on me that this is why the panic had caught up. I realized that I would have to let it run its course. For me, there was no self-improvement-fed cure, nor was it medication, which I never took long enough to see effects, that brought me reprieve. In the end, it was time.

There remains the mystery of why I began to run in the first place, whether the panic had begun before I even left home and why it had arrived. I like to think my wanderlust would have dimmed; my misplaced hunger would have become apparent if I'd only known more about Glory's life, but she, too, is a romanticized cure. Over the last few years, I have often imagined Glory as a tragic protagonist in a far more glamorous and gritty story than my own. I imaged Glory as Grandma, the affected narrator, shared my desire to know her through her own fleeting memories. But Grandma and I spoke about other things over our long distance phone calls, our replacement for the conversations we used to have weekly over coffee and pancakes. Often, such conversations began the same, with mystery—the missing fork in my grandmother's room, who took it? *Call the Navy.* But we would get beyond this most days, get to the past. We became close and I looked forward to our conversations. I had brought up Glory often those first years away, but over time she came up less and less as Grandma's memories became more muddled. I think this is for the best.

In the end, I didn't miss the fantasy. It wasn't Glory's story but ultimately reconciliation with family that made me realize what I wanted to know. It ended up being those that I ran from who taught me the only story I could really understand is my own. The panic, no matter its origination, was just the dramatic flourish at the end of a single chapter I might have otherwise ignored.

About the Author

Jennifer Knox is a Fiction Editor at Our Stories Literary Journal and works as a freelance writer, editor and writing tutor. She grew up in Ohio and lives in Texas. She is currently working on a novel entitled Absurd Hunger.

ALL THINGS THAT MATTER PRESS ™

FOR MORE INFORMATION ON TITLES AVAILABLE FROM
ALL THINGS THAT MATTER PRESS, GO TO
http://allthingsthatmatterpress.com
or contact us at
allthingsthatmatterpress@gmail.com

CPSIA information can be obtained at www.ICGtesting.com
Printed in the USA
LVOW07s1406020715

444749LV00003B/561/P

9 780984 259427